P9-CMP-664

Assessing the
National Curriculum

ASSESSING THE NATIONAL CURRICULUM

edited by
Philip O'Hear and John White

P·C·P
Paul Chapman
Publishing Ltd

Selection and editorial material copyright © 1993 Philip O'Hear
and John White. All other material © 1993 Paul Chapman Publishing,
except as otherwise credited.

All rights reserved

Paul Chapman Publishing Ltd
144 Liverpool Road
London
N1 1LA

Apart from any fair dealing for the purposes of research or
private study, or criticism or review, as permitted under the
Copyright, Designs and Patents Act, 1988, this publication may be
reproduced, stored or transmitted, in any form or by any means,
only with the prior permission in writing of the publishers, or
in the case of reprographic reproduction in accordance with the
terms of licences issued by the Copyright Licensing Agency.
Inquires concerning reproduction outside those terms should be
sent to the publishers at the above mentioned address.

British Library Cataloguing in Publication Data
Assessing the National Curriculum
    I. O'Hear, Philip II. White, John
    375

    ISBN 1 85396 232 5

Typeset by Hewer Text Composition Services Ltd, Edinburgh
Printed and bound by Athenaeum Press, Newcastle upon Tyne

A B C D E F G H   9 8 7 6 5 4 3

Contents

Abbreviations Used in the Text

APU	Assessment of Performance Unit
AT	Attainment Target
BTEC	Business and Technology Education Council
CDT	Craft, Design and Technology
CPVE	Certificate of Pre-Vocational Education
DFE	Department for Education
ERA	Education Reform Act 1988
GCE	General Certificate of Education
GCSE	General Certificate of Secondary Education
gNVQ	General National Vocational Qualification
HE	Higher Education
HMI	Her Majesty's Inspectorate
HMSCI	Her Majesty's Senior Chief Inspector
ILEA	Inner London Education Authority
IT	Information Technology
JMB	Joint Matriculation Board
LEA	Local Education Authority
LMS	Local Management of Schools
NCC	National Curriculum Council
NVQ	National Vocational Qualification
SAT	Standard Assessment Task
SEAC	Schools Examination and Assessment Council
SEN	Special Educational Needs
TA	Teachers' Assessments
TGAT	Task Group on Assessment and Testing
TVEI	Technical and Vocational Education Initiative
YT	Youth Training

Notes on Contributors

Michael Barnett is Professor of Technology and Education at the Institute of Education University of London, having previously spent 25 years at Imperial College, London, concerned with aspects of physics and engineering.

Paul Black is Professor of Science Education at King's College, London. He was co-director of the DES project for national monitoring of science performance (APU) from 1978 to 1990. In 1987 he was appointed chairman of the Task Group on Assessment and Testing. He subsequently served as deputy chairman of the National Curriculum Council until 1991.

Eric Bolton is Professor for Teacher Education at the Institute of Education University of London. Prior to that he was one of Her Majesty's Inspectors of Schools for almost 20 years. From 1983 to 1991 he was Senior Chief Inspector, head of HMI in England and Wales, and much involved in the events and work leading to the 1988 Education Reform Act.

Martin Buck is currently Inspector with Ealing Education Department, having previously been Deputy Head of a London secondary school. He is co-author (with Sally Inman) of *Curriculum Guidance I: Whole School Provision for Personal and Social Development* (1992).

Caroline Gipps is Reader in Education at the Institute of Education University of London. A primary teacher, psychologist and researcher by training, she has carried out a wide range of research on the uses and impact of assessment; she has published both in this area and in the critical evaluation of assessment developments. She is President of the British Educational Research Association in 1992–1993.

Jagdish Gundara has been Head of the Centre for Multicultural Education at the Institute of Education University of London since 1979. His publications include *Racism, Diversity and Education* (ed. with C. Jones and K. Kimberley

(1986) and *Essays on the History of Blacks in Britain* (ed. with I. Duffield) (1992).

Paul Hirst is Visiting Professor in Philosophy of Education at the Institute of Education University of London, having previously been Head of the University of Cambridge Department of Education. A major theorist on the philosophical foundations of the curriculum, he has also been a leading figure in the reform of teacher education.

Sally Inman is currently Tutor for Professional Development in the Initial Teacher Education Department at Goldsmiths' College University of London. She is also Co-ordinator of the Goldsmiths' Centre for Cross-curricular Initiatives and co-author (with Martin Buck) of *Curriculum Guidance 1: Whole School Provision for Personal and Social Development* (1992).

Denis Lawton was until recently Director of the Institute of Education University of London and is now Professor of Education in its Department of Curriculum Studies. He is the author of several books on the curriculum and educational politics, including *Education, Culture and the National Curriculum* (1989) and *Education and Politics in the 1990s* (1992).

Barbara MacGilchrist is a former primary teacher, Chief Inspector, and member of the National Curriculum Council. She is now Head of INSET at the Institute of Education, University of London.

Brahm Norwich is Senior Lecturer in Education, Department of Educational Psychology and Special Educational Needs at the Institute of Education University of London. He has worked as a teacher and educational psychologist. He is the author of *Reappraising Special Needs Education* (1990).

Philip O'Hear is Headteacher of Acland Burghley School in Camden, London. He teaches English and has contributed to national developments in GCSE. Other interests include arts in school, partnership with parents, integration of disabled students, and developing community education. He lectures frequently on curriculum planning, school management and professional development.

Ken Robinson is Professor and Chairman of Arts Education at the University of Warwick. He was principal author of the Gulbenkian Report on *The Arts in Schools* (1982) and from 1985–1989 director of the National Curriculum Council's project on *The Arts in Schools*, which led to a series of publications on *The Arts 5–16* (1992). He is an adviser to the Arts Council of Great Britain.

John Slater was HM Staff Inspector for History from 1974 to 1987 and from 1988 to 1990 was Visiting Professor at the Institute of Education University of London. He recently co-authored *The Aims of School History: the National Curriculum and Beyond* (1992).

John White is Professor of Philosophy of Education at the Institute of Education, University of London. He has written extensively on the aims of education and the school curriculum. His books include *The Aims of Education Restated* (1982) and *Education and the Good Life: Beyond the National Curriculum* (1990). With Philip O'Hear he worked with the Institute for Public Policy Research on their publication *A National Curriculum for All: Laying the Foundations for Success* (1991).

Michael Young teaches in the Department of Policy Studies and is Head of the Post 16 Education Centre Institute of Education University of London. He was a co-author of *A British Baccalaureate: Ending the Division between Education and Training* (1990). His research interests are focused on a project for a Curriculum of the Future as a way of developing a more unified approach to the curriculum at 16-plus.

Chris Woodhead is currently Chief Executive of the National Curriculum Council. He has written numerous books and articles on a range of educational issues. He was one of the 'three wise men' invited by the Secretary of State in December 1991 to make recommendations about the primary curriculum.

Introduction

The National Curriculum has been with us for nearly 5 years. It is an appropriate time to review in the light of experience how successful it has been and what needs to be done to improve it.

Apart from Paul Black's contribution, the present collection of papers grew out of a conference entitled 'The National Curriculum – Which Way Now?' sponsored jointly by the Institute of Education, University of London, Camden Local Education Authority and the Institute for Public Policy Research (IPPR). It was held at the Institute of Education on 1 July 1992.

That conference owed its existence, in turn, to a paper by Philip O'Hear and John White called *A National Curriculum for All: Laying the Foundations for Success* (O'Hear and White 1991). This surveyed the strengths and weaknesses of the 1988 Curriculum and spelt out in some detail a new national curriculum with which to replace it. The paper was background material for the conference and is discussed in several contributions to this book.

Discussion about the National Curriculum since its inception has been at three levels. There has been controversy about whether a national curriculum of any sort is needed at all; about the overall structure of the 1988 Curriculum; and about matters specific to particular curriculum areas. Although there are still eloquent sceptics on the necessity of a national curriculum, most commentators and, it would seem, most teachers now accept the idea in principle. This is true, for instance, of the contributors to this book, none of whom comes out on the other side. The third level, to do with specific objectives in history, English, art, music and other subjects, has been the topic of massive controversy and coverage in the press with the publication of each new Subject Working Party Report or set of Statutory Orders. We are still waiting for the dust to settle in many of these areas.

Most of the discussions in this book are pitched at the second level – about structural features of the National Curriculum. Taken together, they mount a powerful case for the existence of fundamental difficulties in the way in which the 1988 Curriculum was conceived and in favour of its remodelling on more adequate lines. Three criticisms in particular are found in these papers again and again.

The first has to do with the undue dominance of traditional school subjects, often at the expense of content somewhat closer to pupils' lives and expectations – a critique elaborated in different ways in Paul Hirst's call to abandon a 'rationalist' conception of education in favour of a curriculum built around social practices, in John White's plea for a more coherent mapping of underlying values, in Ken Robinson's argument for a reconceptualization of the arts curriculum across the traditional subjects, in Michael Barnett's claim that science teaching should be technology-led, and in Martin Buck and Sally Inman's view that the cross-curricular elements of the 1988 scheme need a more adequate conceptual basis.

The second criticism is that the present curriculum is too tightly prescriptive, laying down mandatory objectives in too much detail. While many of the contributors touch on this, Brahm Norwich explores in more depth the difficulties this creates for the education of pupils with statements of special educational needs; while Barbara MacGilchrist draws attention, among other things, to the 486 statements of attainment that Key Stage 2 teachers may have to take account of.

But the most vociferous objections in this volume are to the current system of National Assessment, especially to the narrowing down of proposals made in the 1988 Report of the Task Group on Assessment and Testing (TGAT) and the moves towards short pencil-and-paper tests. The paragraphs below summarizing the contributions of Denis Lawton, Eric Bolton, Caroline Gipps and Paul Black testify to the consensus among them on this matter.

Critique of the 1988 structure needs to be accompanied by suggestions for alternatives to it and further criticism of these. These are found in abundance in the various essays. As well as authors whose positive suggestions have been already mentioned, Philip O'Hear discusses some of the main reforms put forward in O'Hear and White (1991) while Chris Woodhead rejects many of these point by point. Michael Young urges that the 14–19 curriculum should be conceived as a unitary structure to replace the present academic/vocational divide.

If, as may be hoped, these papers contribute to a fundamental review and perhaps recasting of the 1988 National Curriculum, these tasks depend not only on critique and counterproposal, but also on an objective historical assessment of how and why that curriculum came to acquire the features it did. In the opposing positions on this sketched by Denis Lawton and Eric Bolton (see below), we have the germs of a historical controversy on which we may expect more light to be thrown in the course of time.

At the heart of the disagreements in this book, whether historical as between Lawton and Bolton, or over current and future policy as between Woodhead and O'Hear, is a debate over the need for and/or the possibility of organizing a national curriculum around principles other than subjects. Critics of the 1988 Curriculum attribute many of its problems, such as incoherence, excessive detailed prescription and increasingly reductive assessment, to the lack of a philosophical base from which to determine the detailed structure. Without such a base, these critics argue, the detailed definitions of subjects and arrangements for assessment are open to change and revision, often at the pressure of ideologically motivated lobbies. Defenders of the 1988 scheme argue that only subjects and simple levels for assessment are sufficiently simple, clear and universally understood to be framed in legislation. The majority of the educationists who have contributed to this book incline to the former position. If they are right, then a major challenge for educationists is to articulate, and then win support from parents and politicians for, a clear and comprehensible alternative basis for constructing a national curriculum. We hope this book, with large agreement about the need for clearer aims and values and greater priority on formative student-centred assessment, is a helpful response to that challenge.

We turn now to a more detailed look at each contribution in the order in which it appears.

John White takes off from what O'Hear and White (1991) say about aims and values. He points up the contrast between the 1988 Curriculum and the O'Hear/White version, the former emphasizing knowledge objectives but saying little about the aims they subserve, the latter starting out from an array of values associated with its key aim of preparing students for liberal democratic citizenship and deriving knowledge and other aims from these. He suggests that while in one way the 1988 Curriculum is 'redolent with values', little has been done to order these into a coherent whole. To do so should now be a major task of the National Curriculum Council (NCC). In engaging in it, the NCC should be wary about alleged connexions between moral values and religious belief implicit in recent official pronouncements on values in the National Curriculum.

In his contribution, Philip O'Hear develops and updates the O'Hear/White critique of the 1988 National Curriculum whilst outlining the alternative framework proposed there. The lack of aims, values or organizing principles above the level of subjects leaves the 1988 structure wide open to arbitrary prescription and continued incoherent revision in the face of pressure-group lobbying. The narrowing and destructive tests now being developed represent a victory for those ideologically committed to an elitist and selective structure for education. Only root and branch reform can achieve a national curriculum suited to the needs of future citizens of a liberal democratic, technologically advanced and economically successful society. O'Hear concludes by suggesting that, by working with parents and students to create a coherent curriculum at school level, 'we can build a substantial platform for the changes that are needed'.

Chris Woodhead, Chief Executive of the NCC, responds vigorously to the critique mounted by White and O'Hear. He examines in some detail the alternative they propose and suggests that the less prescriptive framework would undermine the aim of a guaranteed entitlement. He defends the aims set out for the National Curriculum in the Education Reform Act (ERA) and suggests that, for all their philosophical objections, the detailed curriculum proposed by White and O'Hear is similarly composed of subjects and skills. He accepts that 'further work is needed on the 10-level concept' but defends this basic assessment structure as necessary for simplicity and clarity. Whilst agreeing that 'the formative purposes of assessment are of central importance', he denies that these necessarily conflict with the use of assessment information to indicate 'a school's effectiveness'. Research by the NCC shows that the clear guidance has been welcomed whilst changes and revisions made have been in the light of feedback. Through this process, 'specific problems of intellectual coherence and manageability can be addressed', avoiding the damaging confusion of radical change.

While acknowledging that 'never before has there been such an impressive critical statement of common curriculum objectives', Paul Hirst has doubts not only about the wisdom of prescribing such objectives in tight detail, but also about belief in the centrality of the foundation subjects. He contrasts the 'rationalist view' of education, which lies behind this belief and sees knowledge and its application as providing all that is needed in children's education, with the view, which he himself espouses, which 'sees the best available practices of living as foundational, to which subjects are adjuncts and of secondary, specialist significance. On this second view a critical, reflective mastery of practices is what a common curriculum must be about.' The place given to cross-curricular themes in the National Curriculum is some recognition of the importance of this mastery.

Denis Lawton's paper is partly historical, looking back on what he sees as the over-hasty origins of the National Curriculum and the ensuing problems it faced. Examining in detail the reasons for the latter, he identifies the ideological differences within the Conservative Party which led to a curriculum based on conventional subjects rather than on Her Majesty's Inspectorate's (HMI's) 'areas of experience'; the failure to take account of curriculum experts and to begin from the professional concerns of teachers; and the absence of adequate implementation strategies. Like other contributors, he locates a major weakness of the National Curriculum in its assessment system, regretting that the TGAT concept of Standard Assessment Tasks (SAT) is giving way to short pencil-and-paper tests and, more generally, wishing to restrict National Curriculum assessment to formative and diagnostic purposes rather than the monitoring of standards.

Lawton's view that the introduction of the National Curriculum was a political 'quick fix' is not shared by Eric Bolton, who, as Chief HMI during that period, played a leading role in deliberations on the topic. 'It is wrong to suggest that there was no coherent philosophy behind the curriculum that emerged.' Its leading ideas were based on the notions of breadth and balance such as those found in the 'areas of experience' and built on Keith Joseph's Paper *Better Schools* (DES 1985a). The 1988 Curriculum was structured around school subjects because the drafting of legislation needs to be as unambiguous as possible and a structure based on, for instance, areas of experience would have failed to meet this demand. By and large Bolton sees the National Curriculum as working out fairly well – except in one area. The drive towards external pencil-and-paper tests at the expense of teacher assessment threatens to put the assessment cart before the curriculum horse. In the light of US experience of test-led curricula this could be disastrous.

Anxieties about assessment raised by Lawton and Bolton are also prominent in the papers by Caroline Gipps and Paul Black. Gipps begins with a lucid account of the new structure for assessment and recording. She shows in detail how the TGAT model was undermined by the move towards less time-consuming tests, concluding that 'attempts to move towards a new, broader model of assessment . . . have been thwarted.' She sees this administration as using assessment to gear up the educational system and force accountability on schools. Like Lawton, Caroline Gipps doubts whether a single assessment system can both meet formative/diagnostic purposes and provide public information on the performance of schools. She sees recent Scottish experience of assessment as 'weaker on the accountability side and stronger on the professional side' than developments elsewhere in the UK.

Paul Black was the Chairman of TGAT and has also been a member of the NCC. We include here his hard-hitting Presidential Address to the Education Section of the British Association Science Festival '92. In it he castigates the 'sweeping and hurried change' that has occurred in National Assessment with the demise of the TGAT Report. He upbraids the present administration for failing adequately to monitor the new programmes and for basing policy on political prejudices rather than evidence. He describes recent moves in the US away from short standardized tests and towards tests of performance closer to good classroom practice. In many ways leading US ideas on assessment are now very close to the thinking of TGAT and that of the Assessment of Performance Unit (APU) which lay behind it.

Jagdish Gundara explores the notion of entitlement as it applies in a culturally diverse society. Truly comprehensive schools, adequately resourced and working in partnership with local communities, are essential. Such schools could contribute to a common civic culture, a secular 'nest' in which diverse values can flourish without division and breakdown. This approach requires the establishment of a broad values education at the centre of curriculum planning. Religious education (RE) should provide a wide and critical under-standing of the diversity of religions and values in society, respecting the distinction between the public and private domains. Educators need urgently to work towards this to counter the vacuum created by pressures towards atomized values, fundamentalism and empty individualism. We can begin to achieve this by focusing our implementation of entitlement on the real needs of students for a wide values education rather than the narrow curriculum assessed through the National Curriculum tests.

Brahm Norwich's paper concerns the tension between the principle of a common entitlement and that of meeting individual needs. He examines how the National Curriculum affects pupils with Statements of special educational needs (SEN), in both special and ordinary schools. The central prescriptions of the National Curriculum have made it hard for schools to tailor them to the needs of many children with learning difficulties, often leading to formal and informal exceptions and disapplications. The way forward is to distinguish between a broad common curriculum framework of aims and goals and a specific operational version of it like the 1988 National Curriculum. Schools should be able to meet common demands in more flexible ways, thus reducing the need for exceptions. Like Gipps and Lawton, Norwich favours the separation of formative assessment from a system designed for summative/evaluative purposes.

The next four contributions each focus on a particular area of the school curriculum.

In the first, Michael Barnett argues the need for greater coherence between science and technology. Historically, there has been a chasm between the two, science having become a high-status component of a liberal education, with craft – emerging later into craft, design and technology (CDT) – remaining a vocationally-orientated and less prestigious subject. Barnett is attracted by the idea of a technology-led version of the science/technology relationship, wherein science appears in the curriculum largely as a function of its applicability to technology, with special reference to technologies significant to modern industry. He argues cogently for this and examines various problems of curriculum design which flow from it. From his perspective, the 1988 National Curriculum, with its sharp divisions between subjects, 'represents several steps backwards'.

In Ken Robinson's view, provision for the arts in the National Curriculum is 'radically incoherent'. A political agenda that puts more weight on a narrow conception of intellectual attainment than on cultural identity works against them. Despite the impressive strides which arts teaching has made over two decades, 'the spirits of many arts teachers are at a low ebb'. In his essay, Robinson explores what scope there is for imaginative curriculum development within the present framework and favours a new conceptualization of the arts and relationships between them to replace the five art forms around which the current incoherent structure is built.

Martin Buck and Sally Inman offer an account of personal and social development in the National Curriculum. Despite the ERA aims of breadth, balance and relevance to present and future lives, they find no coherence or systematic challenge in the NCC reports on the cross-curricular themes. In the absence of adequate national guidance on the place of personal and social development in the taught curriculum, schools will need to create their own mechanisms for a coherent and sustained approach. Buck and Inman summarize a framework for this which they have developed at Goldsmiths College. This offers pedagogical criteria and issue-based questions around which challenging and coherent sequences of work can be developed. Like many of the contributors, Buck and Inman hope that their work will support 'a new and sustained movement to develop a truly broad and balanced curriculum for all pupils.'

Finally, the humanities. John Slater begins by looking at how they are defined in schools, usually as embracing history, geography and RE, and at different ways schools promote relationships between these. He examines the implications that recent changes to the National Curriculum at Key Stage 4 might have for humanities courses post-14 and goes on to isolate those factors which have made for the most effective humanities courses (without reference to Key Stage). In the second part of his essay, Slater concentrates on history in particular, raising questions both about its aims and about its power to humanize. He concludes that he wishes he 'felt more confident that our National Curriculum and its policy guardians will safeguard, or even understand, the humanizing role of the humanities'.

The last two papers look at issues in the education of pupils at both ends of the age-range to which the National Curriculum applies – primary children, and students of 14 and over.

Drawing on recent reports and research evidence, as well as first-hand experience of schools, Barbara MacGilchrist examines the impact of the National Curriculum on primary education. The culture of the primary school has been challenged, far more than that of the secondary, at the very root. MacGilchrist outlines the changes and their impact on schools: the end of the need to 'invent the curriculum', the new stress on science, history and geography, the stimulation given to teamwork and whole-school planning. At the same time she points to the lack of overall coherence, the constant moving of the goalposts, the need to create time for planning and for sharing subject expertise. She reviews the evidence – such as it is – on the effects of the National Curriculum on children's learning and comes out strongly in favour of a stronger focus on numeracy and especially literacy in the earliest years.

Michael Young opens by declaring that 'the problem with the 14–19 curriculum in this country is . . . that it does not exist' for most young people. Low success rates at 16 and even lower participation beyond it are products of a structure geared to selection and higher education. Reform of the assessment and curriculum structures are both needed. These should enhance the value of Records of Achievement, reduce the importance of external assessment at 16 and provide a coherent but flexible curriculum from age 14 to 19 which combines academic and practical work for all. Professional initiatives, making use of the recent trend towards greater participation by students and the development of non A-level routes to higher education, can achieve more coherence and continuity, despite structural developments in the opposite direction. Optimistically, such student and teacher-led change will create a situation where 'the possibility of real continuity in the 14–19 curriculum could even become a reality.'

1

What Place for Values in the National Curriculum?

John White

The structural weakness of the 1988 Curriculum is plain. Its basis is the 10 foundation subjects. What these are all supposed to be *for* has never been made clear, beyond the virtually uninformative prescription in ERA that they are to promote the 'spiritual, moral, cultural, mental and physical development of pupils' and prepare them for adult life. A more sensible way of working out a national curriculum would have been to begin with a well-worked-out set of aims and only then ask what would be the best vehicles to realize them – *without* assuming that the only vehicles would be those found in the timetabled curriculum, and *without* assuming that the first and main thing to go for would be the traditional school subjects, rather than other ways of organizing learning.

When it became clear that there are important aspects of education not likely to be covered in the basic structure, the cross-curricular themes were bolted across the foundation subjects. Once again, though, the relation between these new elements and underlying educational aims was never spelt out, and the list of themes is arbitrary. Further, it has been assumed, on no good grounds, that the obvious vehicles for promoting citizenship, health education and the rest are the foundation subjects themselves. Lastly, since the themes have no statutory force, they are evidently seen by the authorities, and meant to be seen by others, as of less importance than the foundation subjects, although, once again, no good reason has been given for this.

In our 1991 paper *A National Curriculum for All*, Philip O'Hear and I set out an alternative structure which avoided these weaknesses. In his contribution to this volume, Philip O'Hear says more about the main features of our argument. Here I shall concentrate on just one part of it, about aims and coherence, merely highlighting some central points before taking the argument further.

There is no particular virtue in a national curriculum as such: everything depends on what *kind* it is. A national curriculum can be used as a means of repression or indoctrination, as happened under Hitler and Stalin. In our paper,

Philip and I begin from the central aim of preparing students to become citizens of a liberal democratic society. We do not interpret this narrowly, as learning about voting and other such political matters. These come into the picture, but more basic than them is the aim of passing on the core values of our kind of polity. Central among these is the value of self-determination. We all rightly take it as read that individuals should be freed, as far as practicable, from constraints of poverty, drudgery, ignorance, domination and fear which might hold them back from choosing a worthwhile life of their own. Balancing this, since we are not in the business of producing a nation of autonomous egoists, is an array of values to do with what binds us to other people – from more intimate values like friendship, through shared activities and attachments to local and national groupings, to more impersonal demands of benevolence, justice, respect for others' rights, and a concern for humanity in general.

In the paper we spell out these values in more detail, stressing also the values of self-knowledge – which become increasingly important as students grow towards adolescence – to do with reflectiveness about one's values and the resolution of conflicts between them.

The 1988 Curriculum lays great emphasis on the acquisition of knowledge and understanding, but without making it clear why this is important. For us, too, it is a major objective, but only because it is required by an induction into democratic values and the personal qualities that this fosters. The self-determined life requires a broad understanding of the options, vocational and other, which are open to one, of the obstacles in the way of success, and of the society within which one is making one's choices. Most of the foundation subjects – and more besides – can have a role in providing this understanding. Similarly, to take another personal quality based on a democratic value, a concern to promote the material and non-material well-being of others in one's national community requires some understanding of what this national community *is*, geographically, historically, socially and economically. Understanding its economic structure requires a grasp of technology, science and mathematics. And so on. I perhaps do not need to labour further the dependence of knowledge objectives on underlying ethical values. The main point is that any viable national curriculum should rest on a solid basis of ethical values, and in the interests of overall coherence show how these generate intellectual and other objectives, both large-scale and specific.

Structurally, as I have said, the National Curriculum is weak. It may *look* strong, with its rigid subject structure and detailed statutory demands. But this could be the illusory strength of a blind Cyclops which cannot see which way it is going. Something will have to be done to make the National Curriculum more coherent. More work needs to be done on spelling out underlying aims and working out how these are to be realized in subjects and in themes. A stronger structure is often a more flexible one. It would be good to see less attention paid to prescriptions at the periphery – the detailed statutory requirements of programmes of study and statements of attainment – and more paid to central aims and values.

I was pleased to see some movement in this direction in an article in the *Times Educational Supplement* (29 May 1992) by David Pascall, Chairman of the NCC. Talking of the spiritual and moral dimensions of education, he points out that these pervade the entire Curriculum. 'Now that the statutory framework of the National Curriculum is complete', he writes, he wishes to highlight the ERA aims of promoting pupils' spiritual, moral, cultural, mental and physical development. 'In our classrooms these issues have not always been given the priority they deserve and are often considered controversial topics. But schools cannot be neutral in these areas. Education never has been and never can be value-free.'

So the spotlight is now to be on aims. But what does this entail? We cannot go on for much longer trying to milk an underlying philosophy from the one line in ERA about promoting spiritual, moral and other forms of development. A fuller account of underlying aims and values is called for.

Unfortunately, it is just at this point that David Pascall opts out. He goes on to say: 'I should also emphasise that it is not for the NCC to advocate an evangelical crusade or to publish glossy brochures about core values. All of these issues are for decision and implementation at local level.'

He does not say *why* decisions about values should not be made centrally. These need not involve anything so heady as an 'evangelical crusade', only a further spelling out of what ends the foundation subjects and themes are there to serve. This is essential if the National Curriculum is not to become ossified in the way its equivalents have been in some other countries and if it is to mesh with students' personal, social and civic needs.

In any case, David Pascall is wrong in his implication that the NCC leaves value issues to localities and has nothing to do with recommendations from the centre. If we look at its published material, we see that the Working Party reports for the different subjects all have broad statements of aims for their particular area and all of these incorporate values. A few examples from reports in history, English and art are: imaginativeness, aesthetic sensibility, critical thinking, pleasurable activity, independence, confidence, self-knowledge, tolerance and respect for cultural variety, objectivity. The booklets on cross-curricular themes add further values: for instance, a concern for human rights, as these are affected by economic conditions, the protection of the environment, co-operative activities in economic and environmental areas, fairness, non-violence in resolving conflicts, self-respect, honesty, social stability, 'the paramount importance of democratic decision-making', freedom of thought, freedom from discrimination. There are many further examples. These values are far more determinate than the generalities of the ERA aims. As such, they are more useful in helping to shape more specific objectives.

The National Curriculum is, indeed, redolent with values. A major defect in it is that no one has tried to get them into any kind of order. In the absence of any intelligible structure to bind them together, they tend to be overlooked in favour of knowledge objectives where such a bonding is more evident. The next major task for the NCC is to engage in this task of value-ordering. It needs to establish priorities, to work out what the central values of the National Curriculum should be and how these are related to subordinate values. It could do worse than start from the sketch put forward in O'Hear and White (1991), even if, as is certainly the case, this needs amending in all sorts of ways. But however it goes about it, the NCC could – and should – come up with a new and detailed account of the aims and values that should be demanded of schools.

It could pave the way to this by removing some of the inconsistencies among the values embodied in the National Curriculum. The most telling example of this I know has to do with citizenship. Education for citizenship is one of the cross-curricular themes. Students are to do work on communities, a pluralist society, civic rights and responsibilities, the family, the political and legal systems, work and leisure, the public services. All this involves a lot of understanding of their own society. Among the foundation subjects a notable absentee is social studies – a subject obviously well suited for this purpose. In its absence, history is one of the more helpful vehicles to promote an understanding of society. Yet, apart from a one-term module on the causes of the Second World War, students can leave school knowing nothing of the history of the 20th century. So there are conflicting messages: on the one hand, understanding your own society is important to you as a citizen; on the other, social studies and the recent history of your own society – as distinct from, say, medieval England – are not important enough to be part of your compulsory learning. Citizenship is both important and neglectable.

Removing such inconsistencies, identifying and prioritizing values is a complex task, to which the NCC should now be devoting a large part of its energies. There is no short cut. To judge by some of their recent pronouncements, however, it looks as if the Secretary of State for Education and the Chairman of the NCC may think there is. John Patten has spoken of the role of religion in motivating students to be morally good. David Pascall, in the article referred to, is interested especially in the spiritual and moral dimension of education, stating that 'spiritual growth in this context does not apply only to the development of religious belief but involves encouraging our children to appreciate what is right and wrong, to search for meaning in life and values by which to live.' The more the National Curriculum has focused on knowledge objectives, the more tempting it has come to seem in some quarters to treat the spiritual and moral domains as very closely interconnected and to see religious education as a major way of filling the values vacuum.

There is a lot of cloudy thinking in this area which needs to be dispelled.

First problem. What *is* this 'spiritual development' which is now a statutory aim and which is to pervade not just the RE lesson but the whole Curriculum? For David Pascall, as we have seen, it includes both the development of religious belief and moral learning. Does this mean that 'moral development', despite its distinct slot in the ERA aims, is not, after all, in a separate category from spiritual development, but falls under it? Again, some people associate spirituality not with religion or with morality but with aesthetic values; other people, with all three domains. The fact is we are dealing with a term whose meaning is almost totally unclear and which might well not have come to befog educational debate as it has done recently but for its inclusion in ERA. If we use the word at all, we should make it very evident what we mean by it.

Better, we need clearer, less ambiguous concepts to talk about values. This is why I say that the more determinate value concepts found in NCC documents are more useful to us than terms like spirituality. If I am told, as a teacher, that I have to promote imaginativeness, self-confidence, tolerance and co-operative activity, which are, it is true, not altogether straightforward aims, at least I am given some sense of direction and can embody these values in curriculum activities and other procedures. But if I am told to develop spirituality, what on earth do I do?

A second issue, arising out of the first, is: insofar as one facet of the promotion of spirituality is, as David Pascall states, 'the development of religious belief', is the latter an acceptable aim of school education? Indoctrinating children in religious, political or other beliefs is at odds with bringing them up to be the autonomous agents required by the democratic ideal. How does developing religious belief in them differ from indoctrination?

This leads us into a third issue. If being morally good requires one to be a religious believer, then so does the democratic ideal itself. RE then becomes a cornerstone of a democratic education. Leaving aside conflicts here, just referred to, with the ideal of autonomous agency, there are well-known objections to the claim that morality is dependent on religious belief. Since Hume, attempts to show that moral values are grounded in religion have foundered when one looks in detail at the logic of the argument. Suppose one argues, for instance, as devotees of most religions have for millenia, that one ought to tell the truth, respect others, etc. [call this statement q] because God wants these things or has laid them down in his commandments [statement p], then how can q be derived from p? The latter is a statement of alleged fact. How do we get from a purely factual statement, which says nothing about what *ought* to be the case, to one, like q, which contains an 'ought'?

Why should the fact that God commands us to do something give us a reason to do it? Suppose God commands us to kill our every second child or to lie whenever this suits our interest: ought we then to do so?

If these examples are ruled out of court on the grounds that a Christian, or Jewish, or Muslim God would never demand such things, then when God tells us to tell the truth and respect others, are we morally obliged to do these things *merely* because he says so, or because what he tells us to do is right and good and not wrong and bad? If we say the latter, then, as Plato suggested in *The Euthyphro*, should we not conclude that moral values are, after all, logically independent of religion?

Of course, one might accept this independence and yet argue, like Mr Patten perhaps, that religious belief can still *motivate* children to be morally good, e.g. by urging on them the fear of hellfire for wrongdoing. Leaving out of account the rather weighty assumption that hell, God etc., actually exist, how far such a policy might succeed in making children conform outwardly to moral prohibitions on stealing, lying, physically harming etc., I don't know. I suspect we have moved too far into the era of reflectiveness for it to cut much ice with many. But even if it did work with some, its appeal would be wholly to their self-interest in the shape of avoiding eternal pain: if being morally good at a level deeper than outward conformity has to do with caring for others, with limiting one's own interests in the interests of others, then such a policy would not do much for moral goodness.

Even if religious belief *could* morally motivate, there would still be the further question whether it was the only vehicle for this purpose. The answer is clear. The great majority of British children are brought up on secular lines and we have no reason to think that all of them end up morally bereft. On the contrary. Secular moral education is not perfect, but with a century and more both of experience and of theory behind it, it brings up people – most people – who by and large care for those close to them, are moved by sufferings or injustices at the more impersonal level, and would never dream of stealing or physically harming others.

True, more needs to be done to help people to make sense of their moral worlds, to cope with the conflicts they contain, and to possess the often complex factual understanding which some moral decisions require. That is where the National Curriculum might have achieved so much if its value dimensions had not been neglected.

But there may still be time to do something. Attention could now be focused on what the National Curriculum should be for, on what values it should subserve, and on how its component parts could best promote these values. This is a complex task, not the simple matter it may seem to some of highlighting spiritual development and putting more muscle into RE.

We may not now be able to rebuild the National Curriculum from scratch. But we might be able to improve it bit by bit, like a ship rebuilt at sea – provided we have a better ethical design by which to do so.

2

Coherence in Curriculum Planning

Philip O'Hear

In the previous chapter, John White has pointed up some of the fundamental and unanswered questions raised by the present National Curriculum. He has focused on issues of values and aims since it is central to our argument that the core of worthwhile curriculum planning must be to set aims and values at a level prior to discussion of content. Starting from adequately developed aims about education and its place in our society, there is not only a strong case for a national curriculum but a coherent direction for developing it which will resolve the issues that are presently causing major problems in our planning, such as what to prescribe and what to guide, the role for subjects and topic work, the extent and place for student choice and the shape and nature of the assessment instruments. There is almost universal agreement among the contributors to this book, despite many serious differences about aspects of content and purpose, that the present assessment procedures have the potential to do enormous damage. I want to suggest that this is only a symptom of a more fundamental malaise in the present National Curriculum and that we have an urgent need to reconsider the whole enterprise in order to create the coherent and consistent system for planning and assessing the curriculum that our students – and our nation – both deserve and need.

Drawing on the detailed proposals presented by John White and me in O'Hear and White (1991), I will outline the structure we propose and develop a critique of the present situation. An adequate and successful national curriculum would set curriculum planning at a national and school level in the context of coherent and clear aims and values. Central to our society and its well being is the idea of liberal democracy. Drawing on this ideal and its prime values of self-determination and the recognition of our interdependence on each other, we can articulate the personal qualities needed for a self-determined and socially aware life. These personal qualities are the preconditions of citizenship in a liberal democracy and thus part of the entitlement and obligation of each citizen. We classify them into three broad areas:

personal concerns (managing one's own needs, pursuing personal projects, developing qualities of character);

social involvement and concern for others (working for shared goals, enjoying friends, family, developing more general social responsibility, refraining from harming others, being impartial);

critical and reflective awareness (self-knowledge, including openness, reflectiveness about priorities among one's values, critical awareness and so on).

All these personal qualities have an educational dimension in that their development requires the systematic acquisition of knowledge, understanding, attitudes and competencies. Since possession of them is a fundamental requirement for self-determining and socially responsible participation in a liberal democratic society, it is quite proper that these values should inform our education planning, both nationally and in schools. Moreover, we can draw up a framework for the curriculum, derived from the personal qualities, that includes the *content* of the curriculum, *the wider curriculum* within the life of an effective school, a *structure for progression and choice*, and the *system for assessment and recording*.

Because this framework is at a higher conceptual level than any of the specific details of the operational curriculum, it provides a focused and coherent set of reference points against which to make the decisions of selection, structure and emphasis involved in operational planning. The lack of such a conceptual framework in the present National Curriculum lays it open to the arbitrary backtrackings and pressure group hijackings that have characterized the first five years of its implementation. The case for reform is increasingly urgent as the effects of the destructive and politicized imposition of crude and narrowing assessment instruments become apparent. It is significant that, within this book, two of the chief architects of the present National Curriculum, Eric Bolton and Paul Black, express grave concern that their achievements are being undermined by the crude assessment system now being imposed. What is missing from their critique, I would argue, is a recognition that the 10-subject starting point of the present National Curriculum, rather than providing the clear and universally understandable account of the Curriculum required by Parliamentary draftsmen and defended as such by Eric Bolton, is fundamentally inadequate. Without a more satisfactory conceptual base than a simple list of subjects, any curriculum is going to be open to inconsistent change and excessive prescription as different views of learning and national need are fought out in the detail rather than in the original design. The framework developed in our paper is an attempt to show that such a task is both possible and helpful.

In terms of *the content of the curriculum*, we identify the knowledge, understanding, experience of the arts and practical competencies required for possession of the personal qualities. Often the content we describe is familiar, which is hardly surprising since there is very broad consensus about the main elements of compulsory content. Our framework, however, shows the relevance of content to educational and social values and indicates how the selection of content can be based on this relevance and not simply on assertion and whim. For example, full participation in the political process for our society is dependent on some proper knowledge and understanding of the recent history of this society and the world around it, and of the scientific and technological issues and decisions facing it. Modern world history, a grounding in science and in the basis of technology are all therefore essential areas of knowledge. Other knowledge is required for more personal reasons, such as knowledge of options open to one in work and leisure and, at least, access to the specific knowledge required for chosen fields of activity. From arguments of this kind, we develop a framework for content that gives a rational, coherent and focused basis for selecting aspects of subjects and in deciding whether and how to group them and what to make optional and compulsory. We describe the content using the following structure:

Three areas of knowledge and understanding
  Personal;
  Social;
  Scientific and technological.
Here most, but not all, of the current subject content would be remapped, with a slimmer nationally required core to be covered, with considerable scope for local and school choice in addition. The focus and aims for each part of the compulsory content will be clear so we will be free of such nonsense as the restriction of recent history to Key Stage 4 where it is optional, and the arbitrariness of much of the current content.

Experience of the arts
Here all the arts would be included, and the appreciation of the built environment and natural beauty. In our view, the arts are not a different kind of knowledge but a qualitatively different area of experience. A coherent programme for arts education will develop important aesthetic, moral and human awareness alongside induction into major strands of our culture and of the pleasures of life.

Four areas of practical competencies
  Communication and numeracy;
  Physical movement and health and safety;
  Social interaction;
  Planning and organization.
Of course, these areas will principally be taught through other things, but we believe that the profile of these aspects of practical learning should be raised.

We need to move away from a narrow, and often decontextualized, 'skills' approach to see that the development of competencies is the acquisition of significant skills alongside attitudes and knowledge. We cannot manage, let alone enjoy, our lives without these competencies and the proper use of them is fundamental to the social dimensions of a self-determining life. Thus the competencies take their place as the third element of the content of the curriculum.

Content is only part of the framework, since the institutional life of the school is also part of the whole curriculum, along with the structure for progression and the system for assessment. Some commentators applaud the fact that the present National Curriculum leaves schools free to decide their own ethos and values, although the NCC now have suggested that schools should be required to show what their core values are. John White has analysed the NCC Chairman's position fully in his chapter, but I want to examine more closely the reasons why *the wider curriculum of the effective school* should be included in the framework of an adequate national curriculum. We argue, from our essentially democratic position, that schools and individual teachers should have significant freedom of planning and curriculum decision returned to them. It is obviously vital that schools develop their own sense of community in partnership with their neighbourhoods, parents and students, not least because it is at the level of school and local community that conflicting values in a pluralist and socially and ethnically diverse society can be weighed and prioritized. However, the current 'freedom' for schools to develop the 'whole curriculum' beyond the National Curriculum leaves a vacuum in place of a real entitlement. This will extend to values and attitudes as well as to (apparently but falsely value-free) content. Certain principles and practices must pervade the whole curriculum of the school if access to the development of the personal qualities is to be guaranteed for all.

The second part of our framework, therefore, is a proposed requirement that all schools should draw up and publish policies for the following areas of school life which show how they aim to contribute to national and school aims:

the whole curriculum plan;
the code of conduct;
the structure for partnership with students and families;
the involvement of the whole school community in decision making;
the relationship with the local community;
the development of a social life and an extra-curricular programme;
the structures for promoting equal access to learning;
the establishment of interactive styles of teaching and learning
and opportunities for independent learning.

What we are raising here, particularly in the last two areas, is that a national curriculum concerned with values and coherence needs to address issues of pedagogy as well as content. There is, of course, a strong link between the description of content in our framework and this second element because the practical competencies and, indeed, the relatedness of the areas of knowledge, understanding and the arts cannot be achieved without the support of an effective wider curriculum embedded in the life of the school.

A wider national curriculum does not have to be a more prescriptive one. The third element of our framework is a *structure for progression and choice*. Each Key Stage should have a clear focus appropriate to the age and development of the students. At Key Stage 1, for example, this would focus on literacy and numeracy and the foundation of positive learning and social experience, and be free from the present clutter of content that seems currently to be weakening literacy levels still further. By contrast, at Key Stage 4, we envisage a largely modular structure involving vocational and academic learning and linked to a comprehensive post-16 structure. I want to emphasize that a nationally set core programme of study should be just that: a core profile of work for each Key Stage with space for the school to add to it, to decide the structure for delivery and the context in which to set it. This would return to teachers the important role of detailed planning and contextualizing the national agenda in the light of the needs and interests of their students. This is desirable both philosophically (on the basis of self-determination for teachers and the recognition of their professionalism) but also practically. The teacher is, if properly guided, supported and monitored, in the best position to know how to get the best from the students.

Choice should not, however, extend only to those planning and delivering the curriculum. There is no intrinsic conflict between an entitlement curriculum and guaranteed access to the major areas of learning, and real choice for students in their learning. On the contrary, the development of young people for a democratic society requires that they gain experience of making guided but significant choices. We identify four levels of possible student choice within the curriculum:

within a given sequence of work, i.e. choice over the order;
between options in a sequence of work, e.g. a compulsory core task,
    then choice between extension tasks;
between options, where one of a variety of possibilities is required;
between voluntary activities.

All Key Stages should include student choice at the first two and the fourth levels, which are, of course, extremely important as motivators and supports for active learning as well as providing experience of choice. We would want to extend the principle radically, supported by a modular structure of curriculum organization, and argue that 15% of the timetable at Key Stage 3 and 30% at Key Stage 4 should be reserved for options.

Finally, we come to the fourth and ultimately crucial part of the framework:

the system for assessment and recording. It is increasingly obvious to all but the present Government and their small band of favoured education lobbyists, that the present National Curriculum Tests are likely to do enormous damage to the motivation of students and teachers, and to cause a narrowing of the actual curriculum taught and a serious depression of the real standards achieved. In our analysis, this is because aims to do with enforcing the programmes of study, of monitoring and controlling teachers and schools and of driving for the return of selection have dominated the development of the Tests and, even more, their implementation. There is a huge amount of evidence to support this analysis, much of which is explored in more detail in other chapters of this book. I cite here only some of the more glaring examples, including the destructive imposed changes in GCSE, particularly with regard to course-work, the specification of tiered Tests at Key Stages 3 and 4, the continuing policy shifts leading to the sacking of the agencies developing the Tests, and the significant changes in the actual National Curriculum requirements and priorities written through the Test specifications.

The right-wing education lobby, disappointed at its general failure to undermine the consensus about content and good practice maintained in most of the subject programmes of study, has seen the Tests as a wholly adequate vehicle for redefining the whole enterprise on its own terms. The fact that the basis of the present structure is the 'unproblematic' and 'universally intelligible' 10 subjects without any prior set of values or organizing principles means that whoever controls the focus and nature of the Tests can, in fact, control the whole curriculum. We can see this most clearly in English where, despite all the Parents' Charter piety, all 14-year-olds will take Tests in June 1993 on papers, including set books, whose format, style and content are still unpublished in December 1992. This national disgrace, the result of a determination by the Government to superimpose a model of grammar teaching and approach to literature on to the National Curriculum despite its rejection by every one of its own commissions of enquiry into English, is only a more extreme version of what is happening across the whole curriculum.

It is quite wrong to suggest that the two main pillars of the 1988 Education Reform Act – the Local Management of Schools (LMS) and the National Curriculum – work in opposite directions to achieve a constructive balance. The reduction of the Tests to simple and narrow exercises in memory and decontextualized abstraction pulls the whole National Curriculum to the side of encouraging a destructive and selective market in education where an educated elite of students are served well (if narrowly) by a well-resourced elite of academic schools. The needs of neither the majority, nor of our society for a wide, deep and high standard of education for all future citizens, will be served by this. Against this madness, a huge consensus exists among industry, Local Education Authorities (LEAs) (including many under Conservative control) and the despised education establishment, to support the development of a unified system where academic and vocational courses run in parallel and where assessment records success and encourages high quality learning and continued education.

The problems in the present assessment system, however, are not merely the hijacking of the Test development and specification by those committed ideologically to traditional pedagogy and selection. In our analysis, the single 10-level scale is a more fundamental obstacle to an adequate national curriculum. The existence of a single scale continuing across all Key Stages is bound to demotivate and frustrate the average and below, let alone those in Special Schools who remain, euphemistically, 'visiting' strands of Levels 1 and 2 for their entire school career. Such a scale of achievement, defined in terms of the content and potential attainments of a progressive and age-structured linear curriculum, is not the only way to guarantee a universal entitlement to a core curriculum. On the contrary, it often obstructs access to the level of content and skill required for maximum individual success by imposing the later programmes of study, pitched at high levels of skill and concept, on students still struggling with more basic levels of learning. Elsewhere in this book, Brahm Norwich explores this issue more fully.

What I want to stress here is that this criticism is not made out of any negativity about the students of our nation, or about the capacity of raising the standards of their achievements through a clearly defined and criterion-assessed curriculum. We have no doubt at all that criterion-based assessment, from which clear aims and targets can be set for students, has the potential to raise standards considerably. Indeed, there is substantial research and experiential evidence to show just how powerful an instrument for progress the right kind of assessment structure can be. In the ILEA's Hargreaves Report this approach was described as 'units and credits', in GCSE it emerged as Coursework supported by exemplification and practice marking, in BTEC courses it appears as Modules and Competences. An adequate national curriculum must be supported by this kind of integration of teaching and assessing, allowing real information to be given to students and parents, clearly showing what has been learned and achieved and setting targets for future work.

We argue for a system based on redeveloped records of achievement and owned in partnership by school, student and family. The core national programme of study for each Key Stage would be set out as a national attainment profile covering a wide range of potential achievement from basic to very advanced. The level of achievement by the end of each Key Stage would thus be shown by the extent of completion of the profile rather than by a fixed profile, though it would be possible to show broad bands of achievement within the profile. Since a new profile would start with each Key Stage, building on the learning and achievement of the previous one but not carrying forward a summative level of achievement, this system offers better motivation to weaker students without reducing the challenge to the more able. The programme of study (including the Key Stage 3 and 4 options at a variety of levels) and the attainment profile would offer adequate differentiation to provide work at all levels of achievement with content and difficulty levels matched. The present resources now going into the development and administration of the Tests would be redirected to the production of standard assessment modules and moderation to validate the profiles. The original TGAT aims of integrating assessment into the normal teaching programme and validating practical as well as academic work would be restored without the disadvantages of the 10-level scale. This is an ambitious scheme but not beyond a nation that is willing to place its trust in the professionalism of its teachers to maintain fair and accurate records as the basis of assessment. Validation and moderation procedures would therefore be used to sample and check teacher assessment rather than to replace it or police every element. Such a model is well established and accepted as valid in much of vocational education and there is no reason why it cannot be developed reliably in a comprehensive school system.

I have now described all the elements of the alternative framework for an adequate national curriculum proposed by John White and myself. I have also rehearsed and updated our critique of the present National Curriculum and argued that the case for root and branch reform and not simply adjustment is made stronger rather than weaker by recent developments in its implementation. The most recent moves to rewrite subject curriculum for English and, possibly, for history confirm our fundamental analysis of a curriculum rooted in incoherence and ideology and not in acceptable values and purpose. I want to close this chapter by considering two further issues. Why, given the establishment of the present National Curriculum and a government opposed to the views of educationists almost, it seems, on principle, is it worth arguing a case for an alternative? And, since we have to work within the existing structure and do our best by our students, what is the value of an alternative model to those of us working in schools now?

We can approach both these issues by exploring further the first argument. On this view, the system is responding with health and vigour to the Government's changes. Thus the 1988 National Curriculum is largely in place, the new tests are being developed and implemented and teachers are, once more, responding to the challenges posed by late changes to the syllabuses. The new league tables of results have begun to appear and, rather than cause a political storm, the drive for publicly available standards and simple measures of them is greeted with a largely acquiescent silence from parents and the opposition parties. The educational establishment shows increasing outrage and even includes some of its previously fiercest critics, such as Brian Cox, once Black paper author and now defender of the consensual approach to English that he helped to shape. Our very outrage, however, confirms the view of the Prime Minister that his education policies are right, as he stated clearly at the 1992 Conservative Party Conference. His attitude is supported not just by the cheers of party loyalists but by regular poll evidence that public confidence in the Government's handling of education deteriorated during John MacGregor's period as Education Secretary. For a Conservative Government, working with teachers is not a successful populist strategy and we live in times when the Conservative Government needs all the populist sources it can muster.

None of this political context, however, makes the present policies right or even workable. The professionalism of teachers in trying to implement the 1988 National Curriculum and cope with the Tests as well as possible in the interests of their students, does not signify agreement or conviction. Nor does parental and opposition silence indicate informed assent, let alone consent. As the implications of the present policies become apparent, in large-scale failure and distress in the Tests, the removal of aspects of education that have motivated and challenged older siblings, and the reintroduction of mass streaming and selection, so public opinion will change. Only if educationists are ready with a sound analysis of the present and a well worked out alternative can we avoid yet more incoherent change and avoid the risk of, once again, being held responsible for the failure.

Arguing for radical change in the National Curriculum is not, though, simply a matter of defending our position as educationists. More importantly, it is setting out the kind of structure that is needed for personal and national success. The individual citizens of our nation need a broad and high level of education, preparing them for work in a highly developed and technological economy and for life in a complex and open society. Present policies, involving failure and selection and retaining a strongly enforced divide between the academic and the practical, will not serve this need at all. There is a potentially huge consensus across industry, politicians, parents and students for an adequate national education policy. This will have to include coherence and continuity in the curriculum, the right balance of the practical and the student-centred with the theoretical and the teacher-led, a proper validation of the achievements of the whole student and a clear structure of progression through and beyond compulsory schooling. As educationists concerned with individual as well as national needs and success, we need to be ready to provide the detailed case for change that this consensus will demand when the political climate changes. Engaging in debate now – and we hope our original paper and this book are worthwhile contributions – will allow us both to clarify and update ideas and begin to build a consensus for change.

In the meantime, we have to cope with the present. Many of the other chapters in this book suggest how teachers in particular areas are doing and should do this. My concern here is with the shape of the whole Curriculum and its impact on the whole student. As I have argued at some length, many aspects of the present National Curriculum work against a satisfactory shape and create a harmful impact on the student. However, the present National Curriculum is not the whole curriculum and, even though this is not I think an adequate state of affairs in principle, it is a very significant space in which to work in practice. Drawing on our critique and alternative model, we can implement practical policies that create better coherence and progression. We can set the crude National Curriculum reporting firmly in a school-based system that places the student, and family, at the centre of full records of achievement, offering formative feedback, target setting and motivation as well as levels. More ambitiously, we can work with regional consortia to validate core, wider and transferable achievements within the 14–19 curriculum. We can retain an active place for the arts and for social studies throughout the secondary curriculum and retain the maximum space for student choice. We can use resources under LMS to support extension and extra-curricular provision to offer the width and range of opportunities needed to maintain the confidence and success of all our students. By basing practical school-based policy on a fuller and more adequate view of the curriculum and of assessment, we are also drawing parents and students into a fuller understanding, based on actual experience, of a more coherent curriculum. If they see that a better focused and more coherent model of learning and curriculum planning is available, they will be less tolerant of the narrowing and incoherent elements of the present National Curriculum. In this way, I believe, drawing now on an alternative model in order to do better by our present students is one of the most powerful ways of arguing for change at a national level.

The purpose of this book is to support a critical and properly thought out debate on the future of the present National Curriculum. In this chapter, I have set out in some detail an alternative model which, I believe, offers real coherence and a better prospect for national and individual success. By engaging in this debate and refining our alternative model, while also working in our schools to create in practice the coherent whole curriculum our students need, we can build a substantial platform for the changes that are needed. In a recent visit to Russia, I learned that one of the first acts of the Yeltsin government was to lift the compulsory force of the Russian national curriculum so the schools could deviate from it, subject to the agreement of the local Teachers' Council. Successful reform and a coherent national curriculum will depend on educationists winning a similar degree of responsibility and trust in our country.

3

Do We Need a New National Curriculum? A Critique of O'Hear and White (1991)

Chris Woodhead

Philip O'Hear and John White (1991) agree that we need a national curriculum as a safeguard against 'grassroots vagaries of enthusiasm'. They think, however, that the current National Curriculum is excessively prescriptive and they believe that it lacks any proper rationale. They criticize the fact that it is structured in terms of subjects and argue that it undervalues 'the wider curriculum of the school'. They are unhappy about its use of assessment and they assert that revisions to the National Curriculum have left 'teachers, students and parents confused and uncertain'.

It will not surprise you to hear that, while I would not for a moment pretend that the current National Curriculum is in every detail the right national curriculum, I do not fully sympathize with this impressive catalogue of complaint.

My first and most fundamental objection to the O'Hear/White thesis is that I do not believe that a national curriculum based on what they call 'focused objectives' will be much of a defence against the idiosyncrasy of local provision. O'Hear and White want, on the one hand, to ensure that all children have access to the knowledge, understanding and skills they need if they are to participate in a liberal democracy; on the other, they want 'to reduce prescription in order to promote flexibility'. These two objectives are not, of course, necessarily contradictory. I think myself that the National Curriculum could usefully be made less prescriptive. But there is an obvious danger of throwing the baby out with the bathwater, and, in my view, O'Hear and White are driven by their belief in the school as 'a democratic workplace' to do just this.

This is perhaps unfair in that the present pamphlet does not go into sufficient detail to allow any definitive judgement to be made. What we do have, however, is the argument that we must 'return to schools the degree of control over the curriculum and its whole school context that allows the development of a coherent structure and pedagogy'. Leaving aside the question of whether the present National Curriculum does or does not prevent coherence, such references combine with the generalized tone of the discussion of curriculum objectives to make me think that this new national curriculum will be little different from 'the hit and miss curricula of the old laissez-faire system'.

Take, for example, what is said about communication and numeracy. We are offered a list of specific skills which should be developed under this 'practical competence' (speaking, reading, writing, calculating, organizing data, visual and graphical communication, information technology (IT) skills and some competency in foreign languages). Fair enough, but this list is simply accompanied by a somewhat hortatory gloss to the effect that 'all curriculum areas should help to develop linguistic competencies' and that numeracy should be 'reinforced' by work in areas other than mathematics. This, in itself, will not ensure the entitlement O'Hear and White want for our pupils. Neither, given the emphasis they put on local professional decisions, is it easy to see how sufficient detail can be built into the proposed attainment profiles and core programmes of study to guarantee the curriculum coverage which is needed if the aims they articulate are to be realized.

I also have a problem with O'Hear and White's conviction that we need 'to return to first principles that have been evaded by the present government'. It is, as a point of fact, wrong to assert that the ERA pays no attention to the underlying purpose of the curriculum. The relevant paragraph is certainly terse, but it points clearly enough to the essential and complementary aims of any education system: the need, that is, to develop the individual potential of each pupil, and equally to ensure that every pupil (for their own sakes and that of society as a whole) is equipped to make their future contribution to our corporate well being. The actual paragraph reads:

> *the curriculum for a maintained school satisfies the requirements of this*
> *section if it is a balanced and broadly based curriculum which –*
> *(a) promotes the spiritual, moral, cultural, mental and physical*
> *development of pupils at the school and of society; and*
> *(b) prepares such pupils for the opportunities, responsibilities and*
> *experiences of adult life.*

O'Hear and White are not, however, convinced by this. They argue that a revised national curriculum must be grounded in a clear philosophical/political statement which provides a logical justification for the detailed requirements of the programmes of study. It is always reassuring, of course, to feel that specific objectives flow inexorably from predetermined aims, but when I actually examine the revised curriculum which emerges from the rationale O'Hear and White provide, I wonder whether, in fact, the considerable investment of intellectual energy adds up to anything significantly different from the curriculum we have at present.

What they propose is (and to my mind this is inevitable) work in mathematics, science, history, geography and other subjects of the National Curriculum. Key skills are given useful emphasis, but the programmes of study for the current National Curriculum provide plentiful opportunities for teachers to help pupils to develop these 'competencies'. So there is little that is radically different. The rationale itself ('the new national curriculum should be grounded in the values embedded in liberal democracy', and, in particular, upon the idea that 'all citizens should be free, given certain qualifications, to lead their own lives as they see fit') is perfectly acceptable, but, like most statements of general aims, it is couched at such a level of generality that it is, in fact, hard to criticize.

In my judgement, the most purposeful course of action in reviewing the National Curriculum is to agree that a subject-based curriculum reflects the fact that our understanding of the world is organized in terms of logically distinct 'forms of knowledge', to recognize that many teachers and most parents would find it very difficult to accept a curriculum that was not located very firmly in identifiable subjects, and, given this, to ensure that the National Curriculum Orders for the different subjects presents a challenging, intellectually balanced and manageable set of teaching requirements.

I will touch on this latter point towards the end of this paper, but I need first to comment on the O'Hear and White argument that a 'school curriculum is not simply an assembly of content' and that the National Curriculum has been 'abysmally silent' about the importance of 'the school's ethos, its code of conduct, the values and achievements celebrated in its public life, and the nature of relationships embodied in its informal life'. I find it somewhat ironic that O'Hear and White, committed as they are to the ideal of teacher autonomy, should want statutory legislation to intrude into these areas of professional responsibility. Of course a curriculum is more than 'an assembly of content'. The question, though, is whether or not the government should seek through law to determine the context or 'ethos' in which this specified curriculum is taught. I do not myself see how such legislation could possibly be enforced, but, if it could, it would be an extremely unfortunate step. The 'abysmal silence' is a pragmatic and wholly proper recognition that it is for schools to decide the pattern of curriculum organization, the pedagogy and the values which inform their day to day practice.

O'Hear and White believe that assessment within the National Curriculum is marked by 'similar confusions'. They have three specific complaints: first, that 'assessment has been used to enforce the detailed control of the content of each subject'; second, that 'assessment is used to monitor the teacher and the school'; and third, that 'assessment will identify and reinforce failure'.

The use of the word 'control' takes us, of course, back to the earlier discussion about the balance which needs to be struck between national prescription and local autonomy. But, leaving this bigger question to one side, it is entirely logical that SATs are based 'on the sequence and levels of subjects'. Assessment arrangements ought to flow from the structure of the curriculum. It would be distinctly odd if, for example, the SATs in English for 7-year-olds did not assess the understanding and skills which the programmes of study for Key Stage 1 are designed to promote in this subject. The issue, therefore, is whether the sequence of the programmes of study is the right one and whether the tests used provide a reliable and valid measure of pupil achievement given this sequence. Talk of the curriculum being 'controlled' through assessment arrangements simply raises the emotional tone in an unhelpful manner.

While O'Hear and White do suggest that 'achievements recorded in national attainment profiles' (which will replace SATs in their version of the national curriculum) should be included in school inspection reports, the general emphasis of their argument is very much against the reporting of school achievement. The purpose of assessment, according to O'Hear and White, is 'to record and support the progress of individual students and to promote partnership between school, family and student' and they seem to believe that the current arrangements are designed more to control and humiliate teachers than to illuminate pupil progress.

I entirely agree that assessment ought to identify what 'has been learned' and 'what still needs to be learned'. But, as O'Hear and White state, this achievement has to be recorded 'against national and understood targets', and I am by no means convinced that their proposed attainment profiles will provide clear evidence of achievement against national targets which can be readily understood by the general public.

If the concept of a partnership between parent and school is to mean anything, then the parent has a right to know about the school's strengths and weaknesses. Pupil achievement in National Curriculum subjects is a critical measure of a school's effectiveness. Data from assessment tests ought, therefore, to be published in an intelligible form. The issue of whether or not scores should be 'adjusted' to reflect the nature of community which the school serves is a difficult, but second order, question which should not be allowed to confuse the main argument. While, therefore, I agree that the formative purposes of assessment are of central importance, I also think that the data gathered from such assessment provides important insights into a school's effectiveness and should be made available to parents as their children progress through the school system. There is nothing sinister in this. Neither is there any necessary conflict between the use of assessment for these two purposes.

O'Hear and White's third point on assessment is that it will 'identify and reinforce failure'. Again, the language is unhelpfully emotive. All assessment, to use their own phrase, 'identifies what still needs to be learned'. It reveals, that is, what a pupil does not know or cannot do. Whether this amounts to the identification or reinforcement of failure depends on how the school and teacher use the information. I agree that further work is needed on the 10-level concept (any system of criterion-based assessment is, as O'Hear and White recognize, 'difficult to construct'), but it does not concern me that 'the 10 levels are based on the notion of progressive learning'. Is not all learning progressive?

The challenge is to provide a meaningful record of pupil progress. O'Hear and White reject the notion of a 'level' in favour of an attainment profile which gives a full description of the knowledge, understanding and skills which a pupil has mastered. This has its appeal, but could also be pretty meaningless to many parents. In my view, we need a simple and clear approach which can be easily understood, and I am prepared, therefore, to live with the inevitable loss of precision and detail. Such detail can, after all, be communicated through reports and orally at parents' meetings.

O'Hear and White's final criticism is that changes to the National Curriculum have left everyone 'confused and uncertain'. I agree that we face some difficult judgements in deciding whether it is better to revise aspects of the National Curriculum as problems emerge or to live with these problems in the interests of stability. In confronting this issue, NCC has asked two questions: Are the Orders manageable and are they likely to deliver the overall aims of the ERA and raise standards of pupil achievement? The advice we offered to the Secretary of State on the case for revising the Technology Order was based, for example, on our conclusion that the language of that Order is difficult for non-specialists to understand and that the programmes of study (particularly in Key Stage 4) lack focus and rigour. The Order, in short, is difficult to manage and unlikely to raise standards.

In our judgement, these problems were sufficiently serious to demand immediate action. This was a pragmatic decision, taken after listening to a wide range of opinion, and, in particular, to the experience of primary teachers who have had to deal with all National Curriculum subjects. I agree with O'Hear and White that there is a significant measure of 'confusion and uncertainty', and, given the enormous efforts many teachers have made in implementing the National Curriculum, that it is vitally important not to add to their difficulties and undermine the progress which has been made so far.

But progress there has been and the mood is not simply one of confusion. The teachers I talked to this summer [1992] at our primary seminars were, for example, very clear about both the improvements (to the balance of the curriculum and to teaching and learning within individual subjects) which the National Curriculum had brought *and* its weaknesses. On the latter, there was a strong sense that it was difficult in Key Stage 1 to find sufficient time to deal properly with basic skills of literacy and numeracy and that in Key Stage 2 the programmes of study simply asked too much. We will gather further evidence about these concerns over the next few months with a view to offering the Secretary of State advice next Spring.

This, for me, is the way forward. There are certainly problems with the current Orders which need to be resolved. I am not, however, persuaded by the O'Hear and White argument that the National Curriculum is fundamentally flawed or by the new national curriculum which they propose. To follow their arguments would create further and unnecessary uncertainty when we need a period of consultation in which specific problems of intellectual coherence and manageability can be addressed. As an approach, this pragmatic step by step revision lacks the glamour and excitement of a radical philosophical upheaval, but it is likely to prove of more practical use.

4

The Foundations of the National Curriculum: Why Subjects?

Paul H. Hirst

The fundamental concerns of the National Curriculum have in many important respects been clearly set out. From the start it was explicitly stated that the Curriculum aims to provide a broad and balanced programme which 'promotes the spiritual, moral, cultural, mental and physical development of pupils' and which prepares them 'for the opportunities, responsibilities and experiences of adult life' (ERA 1988, Section I). The means to these ends have also been clearly mapped. First there are the 10 basic or foundation subjects, each one directly concerned with some major area of understanding, knowledge and skill, each formulated in terms of staged attainment targets, programmes of study and assessment tasks. To these must be added RE and, as appropriate, optional subjects. Finally there are cross-curriculum elements which are said to make a major contribution to personal and social education, which tie together the broad education of the individual and augment what comes from the basic curriculum. These elements are in part dimensions of learning and skills that are significant across many or all subjects. But there are also important cross-curriculum themes, five of which are identified as essential: economic and industrial understanding, careers education and guidance, health education, education for citizenship, and environmental education (see NCC 1990b).

In this whole plan, most attention so far has not surprisingly been devoted to the spelling out in detail of the distinct foundation subjects and their practical implementation in schools. By contrast the content and place of the cross-curriculum themes has received little public or professional consideration in spite of the issuing of a significant paper by the NCC on each of the five areas listed above. The document on education for citizenship (NCC 1990c), for instance, sets out in quite some detail eight essential components of content, covering the notions of community, roles and relationships in a pluralist society and the duties, responsibilities and rights of being a citizen. These are related to five specific contexts: those of the family; democratic action; the law; work, employment and leisure; and public service. Forms of experience, activity and

study are suggested in which pupils are expected to develop not only understanding and knowledge on many specific personal and social matters, but
skills, positive attitudes and personal qualities essential for life in a democracy,
including a personal moral code embodying particular stated values and beliefs.
There are even examples given of work appropriate to each Key Stage of the
whole Curriculum.

Taking together these theme proposals and all that has been developed for
the foundation subjects, there can be no doubt that as a whole the National
Curriculum is an extremely ambitious enterprise. Never before has there been
such an impressive official statement of common curriculum objectives.
Certainly now there can be no uncertainty about what is expected of
schools, and critics of objectives and of the work of schools have specific
details they must address directly. What is more, initial fears that this whole
project would be very narrowly conceived along academic or strictly utilitarian
lines have been proved ill-founded.

Yet surveying this enterprise and what is already happening in its practical
implementation, two major questions about the very nature of this approach
become progressively more insistent. First, isn't the whole thing so enormously
ambitious that planning rationally for all these detailed achievements is in practice
quite impossible? Are not the compexities of teaching such that it is unrealistic to
think that objectives of these kinds can be coherently pre-structured, effective
means to them pre-determined, and situations then carefully controlled in
practice so as to bring about what was planned? Is there not perhaps something
fundamentally mistaken about conceiving curriculum planning in quite this way?
In practice, expectations have to be slimmed down to what are seen as the
essentials. Exciting syllabuses and programmes, used effectively before the advent
of the post-1988 requirements, are being adapted to the new situation, even if
much hoped for developments are in danger of getting lost. In this process, the idea
in early documents that schools should structure as they like the actual teaching
units in grand new plans has simply got lost. If pre-existing units cannot be
adjusted, schools understandably plan directly for subjects that directly mirror
what the foundation subject programmes demand. The notion that the plethora of
objectives from all the subjects and themes, spelt out in pretty tight detail under
ordered and staged categories, with many of them to be tested under such
categories, could be imaginatively and defensibly reorganized into a scheme to
suit the unique circumstances of particular institutions and individuals is surely
megalomaniac. In fact the idea of flexibility in detailed nationally-controlled
planning is both impracticable and inconsistent with a central assumption
running throughout the National Curriculum proposals. This is the belief that
its major objectives are of their very nature fundamentally structured in a series of
basic subjects around which all the rest we seek can be ordered. No wonder the
pressure is so strong for even the earliest work of pupils in Key Stage 1 to be subject
structured.

But all this only leads to the second question. What is the justification offered for this belief in the importance of a set of foundation subjects which provide the fundamental elements of the Curriculum? The answer, I suggest, lies in the implicit acceptance of a group of doctrines that I will, for convenience, label 'the rationalist view'. On this view, all we want in the education of children, in their personal, moral, cultural and physical development, in their coming to live lives in which they are self-directing, taking on their responsibilities realistically in the contemporary world and so on, is to be found primarily in human knowledge and in the application of that knowledge. To act responsibly in relation to the material world, for instance, is to study it scientifically, to get the best knowledge there is, and then to apply that knowledge in our control of the world, developing the necessary technical apparatus. What we first need is the knowledge, the scientific knowledge, which we will get from physics, chemistry and many other appropriate sciences. We can then turn this into more practically orientated understanding in technology and engineering, and then learn to carry out what we know we must do. Knowledge is the basis, and the best form of living is always the application of knowledge. It is the same in any other sphere. What we need primarily is simply to understand. We need to understand human history and human society in the disciplines which give us that understanding. When we have got that, then we can set to work applying that knowledge to the achievement of the sort of society we want. Again if we want to develop aesthetic capacities, we must study, say, the achievements of painters of the past to understand what is involved in artistic creation. We must learn the skills to apply that understanding and then and only then can we hope to paint successfully. This rationalist approach to the curriculum thus holds that a curriculum is first about understanding, then about skills and attitudes and then about getting on with life. It is thought to work because by these means pupils acquire all the knowledge they need.

But where do we go for the accurate knowledge the Curriculum requires? We go to the standard university disciplines where alone it can be found. It is no good going to common sense as that will provide much falsehood and error about the physical world or human society. We must go to mathematicians, scientists, geographers, historians, those who have the specialist knowledge. When we want skills of application that are important, we must go to the people with specialist skills. They will tell us what it is that everybody ought to have if only at an elementary level. Knowledge is seen as fundamental to everything. It is fundamental to judgement. It is fundamental to skills, to feelings, attitudes and values. Knowledge therefore is what pupils must get above all else and it will be in the traditional established disciplines, where knowledge has been developed in an ordered structured way, that this knowledge is primarily to be found. It is therefore from these subjects and related areas of practical skills that the curriculum must be fashioned.

There is, however, a very different view of what the achievements we seek through the curriculum actually entail. On this view, the rationalist account is considered mistaken as to what the development of knowledge involves, collectively and individually, and how this relates to the other objectives we are pursuing. If we look at how people have in fact developed rational understanding and have come to live reasonable lives, things do not actually fit the rationalist picture. To take the simplest of examples, human beings have not had to wait for scientists to discover what foods are good to eat. It is by practical experience in a thoughtful way that more enjoyable, more satisfying and more healthy foods were first distinguished. Fundamental sciences were not the source of our basic knowledge about foods and indeed could not have been. People must get on with their lives, whether fundamental areas of knowledge are there to assist or not, and most of the significant knowledge we live by has not been generated by academic specialists nor could it ever be. It has come in practical activities and pursuits, by trial and error. We understand the world primarily in practical terms and under concepts devised in that context. We have first learnt collectively, and still first learn individually, to distinguish among foods, not in the terms the sciences provide, but in terms to do with the practical activities of eating, obtaining and preparing food. Whatever science may or may not do to help, our knowledge and understanding of food begins from and is ultimately tested by its consequences in practice. Similarly successful personal and social relationships are first achieved by learning how to relate to others in practice. Here knowledge, skill and appropriate attitudes are achieved together. It is not the case that success comes from the discovery or mastery of knowledge in formal, structured disciplines, in subjects, which is then applied. Of its nature knowledge and understanding is always generated in relation to relevant skills, attitudes and values. These elements come all of a package in areas of human living and not as dismembered items to be discretely mastered and then put together.

But what then of the traditional subjects and disciplines in which so much of our knowledge and understanding seems to be located? Developed relatively late in human history, their generation has surely come about with the search for explanation rather than successful practice itself. It has been achieved by progressive abstraction of different aspects of experience under specially constructed theoretical concepts. It is by abstracting from all other features so as to concentrate on the causal relations of physical objects that major areas of the sciences have been generated. Likewise, by concentrating on the merely psychological or sociological features of human relationships and practices, other abstracted domains of understanding have been developed. By, as it were, pulling these elements out of the complex realities of real life practices and situations, we have created academic practices concerned with the pursuit of knowledge for its own sake, but thereby we have created knowledge dissociated by its very concepts from the pursuits of daily living. Yet if the abstract, theoretical subjects that result concentrate on only limited aspects of our common world they can nevertheless inform us of crucial considerations for the practices of daily life. Knowledge developed in the sciences and other subject disciplines, even taken all together, can never give us all we need to derive what to do in specific concrete terms. Living as a human person, or developing as a person, does not come from learning and applying abstract subject knowledge. It comes in practical experience, by mastering the best practices of living we have. Those practices are not specialist academic practices either, for the role of academic practices is not to provide the basis for living but to provide limited if penetrating insights that can help the practical development of more successful practices. I am arguing that academic subjects are secondary and indirect in their significance for human living. Important though they are for the development of sophisticated advances in living, they are directly of little use to us individually unless we are professional academics or professional generators of new possibilities for social or technical practices. On this view, we will want pupils above all to master the best practices of living available in our society, not academic subjects and specialized skills. The latter are for the few and are not what education is basically about.

I have sketched two opposing views which differ radically in their account of what is fundamental in education. One sees subjects as foundational, to be complemented, topped up, fleshed out with other elements pupils need to master. The second view sees the best available practices of living as foundational, to which subjects are adjuncts and of secondary, specialist significance. On this second view a critical, reflective mastery of practices is what a common curriculum must be about. But if a curriculum were to be planned in terms of such practices what would it look like? Clearly it would seek to follow the major divisions of areas of practice into which we have for convenience come to categorize our living, in relation to the physical world and in personal and social activities. In its first phase the curriculum would be concerned to initiate pupils into the basic practices of contemporary life that everyone needs to master to a significant degree. These can be loosely grouped into some six major areas, though there are clearly complex inter-relations between these and many very varied curriculum organizations are manifestly possible. It is however useful I suppose to distinguish the following:

(a) Practices concerned with coping with the *physical world*, including, for example, necessary motor skills, practices to do with food, health, safety, domestic and environmental circumstances.

(b) *Communication* practices including those of reading, writing, conversing, numeracy and information technology.

(c) Practices involved in the relationships of *personal and family life*.

(d) *Wider social practices* such as those to do with local, national and

(e)   Practices of *the arts and design* as in, say, literature, music, dance, painting, sculpture and architecture.

(f)   Practices concerned with *religious beliefs and fundamental values*.

What would be wanted in all these areas is initiation into real life practices, into what people do, think and feel. It would be a matter of acquiring knowledge, skills, attitudes and values linked together as they have been developed, not as pieced together starting from formal learnings. What we would need to develop is a much more systematic and detailed mapping of practices in these areas, and the development of much more carefully considered ways of introducing pupils to them in relation to their own interests and concerns.

As pupils progress up the secondary school, though the same concern for practices would continue to dominate the curriculum, the approach to them would begin to shift. In this second phase critical reflection on the practices of phase one and much more considered participation in them would replace mere initiation. By examining the significance and consequences of practices, looking at alternative forms of personal and social relationships, pupils would begin to make decisions and choices for themselves on a progressively more informed and thought-through basis. This would involve the development above all of practical reason and relevant elements of theoretical understanding.

In turn this would lead to a third phase in which the curriculum would focus on the development of specialist forms of practice chosen by pupils in the light of their work, leisure or other personal and social interests and their individual abilities. It is here that academic subjects and other vocational pursuits would come into their own, but the range of choices made in this phase is of major significance in the distinctive structuring of the individual's life to which it leads.

The three phases of this curriculum approach, though representing successive emphasis, must not be taken as strictly sequential stages. The need for greater proficiency in basic practices and in new practices based on technological and social developments can mean that phase one activities would continue late in a pupil's school career. The depth of critical reflection of the second phase developed in any area would clearly be a matter of degree and this form of education would be of importance for all, right through and beyond secondary schooling. The balance of emphases on those phases would be a complex matter needing careful consideration for individual pupils. But the character of this curriculum and its pursuits would, I suggest, be common for all and would constitute a defensible form of national curriculum. It would be a curriculum which would in many ways simply invert the emphases in the National Curriculum as we now have it. Instead of making subjects primary and practically oriented themes secondary, it would make initiation into practices fundamental and sustained attention to subjects a matter of personal choice.

But what prospect is there for our moving to a National Curriculum in these terms? Superficially, the rigid imposition of tightly defined subjects in our present approach looks very unpromising and indeed a retrograde step after the much more enlightened curriculum developments taking place in many schools prior to the ERA. Formal academic, specialist demands had begun to give way to much more practice-based work in new curriculum units operating either under appropriate new titles or as reconceived subjects. But a great deal that appears under the cross-curriculum themes of the National Curriculum is the product of these developments. The place given to these themes is thus at least some recognition in the Curriculum of the value of education in social practices of great variety. Again, after significant struggles in different working groups, not all the foundation subjects are quite as tightly cast into the academic mould as many feared. Perhaps all is not lost for the approach I have outlined.

Yet the emphases in current political pronouncements are nearly all on the wrong tack and more adequately informed comments are constantly vilified as expressions of professional self-interest. Still, if subjects can be gradually transformed into more practice-based units, and the importance of the themes brought forward, there is in the existing framework scope for significant change. Responsibly done, such changes would only enhance pupils' education, and parental opinion – a powerful force that is listened to – is not as blindly locked into an obsession with traditional subjects as is often assumed. Many changes in society and indeed in higher education are constantly pressurizing schools into more practice-based work. Sadly, in the short term the National Curriculum may well do little to enhance real education in our schools. But in the long term it may well serve to bring to the fore the fundamentally important issues I have tried to voice. It may also turn out to have instituted the mechanisms that were needed to bring about the enlightened and responsible changes still needed throughout our educational system as a whole.

5

National Curriculum: Professional or Ideological?

Denis Lawton

Introduction

By the early 1980s, there was a good deal of professional agreement that a move in the direction of a national curriculum was needed. Now many professionals are bitterly disappointed and disillusioned. What went wrong?

Background

A national curriculum was not on the political agenda until the mid-1980s. The ideologically different notion of a common curriculum had been on the *educational* agenda for much longer (Council for Curriculum Reform 1945, Williams 1961, Lawton 1973); and HMI had been discussing the desirability of an Entitlement Curriculum from the early 1970s, and especially since *Curriculum 11–16* (DES 1977). But that approach to curriculum planning should also be seen as quite distinct from the 1988 National Curriculum: the HMI strategy would have been persuasion and gentle dissemination rather than the kind of legislation for a top-down curriculum which appeared in 1988.

We may need to look in a little more detail at the years 1979–1992.

First of all, it is not without significance that during those 13 years of Conservative rule, there have been two Prime Ministers and, more importantly, six Secretaries of State for Education:

(1) 1979–1981: Mark Carlisle apparently showed little interest in the idea of a national curriculum, and spent his time struggling to retain a reasonable share of the reducing public expenditure (and carving out enough money for the Assisted Places Scheme).

Copyright © 1993, Denis Lawton.

(2) 1981–1986: Keith Joseph was ideologically opposed to the idea of a national curriculum which was, however, raised for discussion in his time (*Better Schools* (DES 1985a)) explicitly rejected a national curriculum).

(3) 1986–1989: Kenneth Baker was the enthusiast for and driving force behind the National Curriculum. He seized upon the idea eagerly and wanted results very quickly – for reasons we can only speculate about. But the haste was destructive. And, ironically, despite the haste, Baker did not have the chance of putting his plan into operation: he was 'promoted' in 1989 to be Chairman of the Party.

(4) 1989–1990: John MacGregor was left with the job of implementation. He was beginning to appreciate the difficulties and the complexities involved (some say he listened; others say he 'went native'). He was moved on.

(5) 1990–1992: Kenneth Clarke was appointed by Margaret Thatcher to apply the same kind of diplomatic skills to education that had been so successful in the NHS. He wanted common sense simplicity – an end to 'elaborate nonsense'.

(6) April 1992–? John Patten . . . ?

The Education Reform Act 1988 and After

In discussing the National Curriculum, we are really talking about a very brief period, from Kenneth Baker's North of England speech in January 1987 to 1992. Less than 6 years: a short time in education, but a very long time in politics. I keep stressing the time factor because it is such an important part of the analysis of implementation.

On 9 January 1987 Kenneth Baker, as Secretary of State, made a speech to the North of England Conference in Rotherham (DES 1987b). He suggested that the English education system was 'eccentric' – less centralized than that of France or Germany. He complained that standards were not high enough and that there was lack of agreement over a curriculum for the 14–16 age group:

> *These weaknesses do not arise in those West European countries where the schools follow more or less standard national syllabuses. In those countries the school system produces results which overall are at least as satisfactory as those produced here; and the teachers are no less professional than ours. Nor do these countries show any sign of wanting to give up the advantages of national syllabuses. . . .*

That statement was not completely correct: Baker ignored the fact that many countries with centralized curricula (including France) were trying to free schools from too much central control. But, if you take out the attempt at persuasive rhetoric, Kenneth Baker was simply saying that he wanted a school system that was more efficient, with higher standards and with better accountability.

Problems of Devising and Implementing the National Curriculum

There are at least three explanations for the problems that arose:

Ideological contradictions within the Conservative Party.
Operational problems about the National Curriculum: it was bureaucratic, not professional.
Implementational strategies were ignored or not understood.

It may be helpful to look at each of them a little more closely.

Ideological Contradictions

Secretaries of State for Education, like other Cabinet Ministers, but perhaps more so, have to gain support from all sides of the Party. I have elsewhere (Lawton 1989) suggested that there are four (overlapping) ideological positions on education which would have been important for curriculum planning, at least three of which could be found in the Conservative Party in 1987.

Counting from the right:

(a) The Privatizers (who would prefer to abolish state schools and let people pay for what they want and can afford);
(b) Minimalists (who accept the need for state schooling but choose not to use it for their own children, and prefer the state to provide something less expensive – they tend to talk about 'the basics' and see schooling in terms of training for work rather than general education);
(c) Pluralists (who would like state education to be so good that there would be no motive for having private schools – nevertheless they argue in favour of the continued existence of independent schools on grounds of social diversity, freedom of choice and academic differentiation);
(d) Comprehensive planners (who would like to plan for a single system catering for all social and intellectual types of children). If there were any 'comprehensive planners' in the Conservative Party in 1987–1988, they kept their heads down.

A curriculum is often a compromise, but some compromises involve contradictions and confusion rather than coherence. The kind of national curriculum envisaged or regarded as acceptable within the Conservative Party varied according to ideological position; and Kenneth Baker also had to convince his Cabinet colleagues that he had not been corrupted by his department. Thus the National Curriculum *content* was expressed in a very conventional way indeed – a list of subjects that any MP would immediately recognize and regard as 'sound common sense'. The HMI Entitlement Curriculum Model (based on 'areas of experience' rather than subjects) was ignored. It was unfamiliar and looked suspiciously like 'educational theory' – an increasingly taboo concept.

But the 'list of subjects' approach to the Curriculum was considered by most curriculum experts to be quite inappropriate for the 1990s: so many vital issues (for example, health education, political awareness, etc.) were not included in the subject structure; hence the repair work now being embarked upon by the NCC in the field of cross-curricular themes, etc.

Curriculum experts were carefully ignored in 1987; but assessment experts could not be. The different sections of the Tory Party were promised greater national accountability *and* more market competition. A new assessment system was needed which could deliver data demonstrating the efficiency (or lack of it) in every state school, as well as providing test scores which could be used *competitively* and published in league table form. (Thus satisfying minimalists as well as privatizers.) I will return to this under 'implementation'.

Operational Problems

The National Curriculum was bureaucratic rather than professional. (This is not unconnected with the points made about ideology above.) There is a mass of literature showing that successful curriculum change should start from the professional concerns of teachers, making use of their knowledge and experience, not as a top-down plan imposed on teachers by civil servants. Since 1988 teachers have increasingly felt deskilled and demoralized as a result of National Curriculum arrangements. No attempt was made to give them 'joint ownership' of either the Curriculum or its assessment. Teachers behaved very professionally and did their best with the unsatisfactory curriculum model, but although the principle of a national curriculum is now generally accepted, they still regard the 1988 version as something alien which has to be accommodated.

The idea of a national curriculum was a tremendous opportunity: but it was a missed opportunity – largely because teachers were treated as hirelings to be instructed rather than as professionals to be involved at all stages and at all levels. This could easily have been foreseen and avoided. Another bureaucratic mistake was to move from very general aims to lists of contents expressed as objectives (or 'statements of attainment') without any intervening justification or explanation; another serious error of curriculum design which should have been avoided.

Implementation Strategies

We also know a good deal now about problems of ideal and reality: about the dangers of the gaps between planning and the realization of those plans.

In many parts of the world (OECD 1988) hard lessons have been learned about the difficulty of transferring splendid curriculum ideas into practice. The reasons for the difficulties of implementing curriculum change are no longer a mystery: the practical problems are extremely well documented (e.g. Fullan 1982). And it would have been possible to overcome them.

The National Curriculum itself, although very traditional, did involve some difficult changes: e.g. fitting more subjects into the 14–16 timetable, making sure that enough teachers would be available for subjects such as technology and modern languages. Such problems were ignored, and only when the results of the technology curriculum began to be particularly disastrous was action taken to rethink the nature of the subject and how it might be taught by existing teachers.

Even more importantly, from an implementation point of view, the excellent assessment scheme devised by TGAT (DES 1988) should have involved:

(a) adequate time for co-ordination between the Subject Working Groups;
(b) time for making teachers familiar with the new ideas and procedures;
(c) time and resources for adequate training and moderation exercises for both Teachers' Assessments (TA) and Standard Assessment Tasks (SAT).

The most common error in the implementation of curriculum change is to underestimate the time and resources needed. The 1988 National Curriculum will undoubtedly go down in history as a classic case of neglecting the lessons of previous studies.

For the National Curriculum itself, several changes have been made, watering down the idea of entitlement to a new list of subjects with varying priorities. From 14–16, students may now choose to drop either history or geography, and music and art have become completely optional.

Moreover, the National Curriculum Subject Working Groups developed quite distinct concepts of 'profile components' and 'attainment targets' (ATs) which resulted in the mathematics and science ATs having to be reconsidered in 1991; the number of ATs was reduced from 14 and 17 to 5 and 4 – just when teachers were beginning to get familiar with the Mark 1 model.

As for assessment, because of inadequate time and resources the crucial concept of SATs has been distorted and replaced by short tests. Let me elaborate on that particular issue: the TGAT model of assessment possessed a number of advantages, even conceptual innovations of considerable power. Central to the new concept of assessment was the SAT. The SAT was intended to be a form of assessment which would avoid many of the disadvantages of conventional paper-and-pencil tests (not least for 7-year-olds). The idea was that good examples of teaching–learning situations would be used by teachers in a standard way with built-in assessment opportunities for the teachers. Such assessment would not be either disruptive or intrusive. Some politicians (and maybe civil servants) were always suspicious about this approach which was eventually dismissed as 'elaborate nonsense' by Kenneth Clarke and replaced by more conventional tests – with all the disadvantages that TGAT had tried to avoid, and with little hope of validity and reliability.

The Alternative?

So far this paper has been rather negative, criticizing the politicians and some civil servants for their ignorance and impatience. What might have happened with better planning and better advice?

(a) It would have been sensible to have encouraged and extended the HMI experiments with LEAs on school-based curriculum development using the 'Entitlement Curriculum' as a set of guidelines for improving practice.

(b) Assessment could have been introduced over a much longer period, allowing for the work of the individual Subject Groups to be co-ordinated, rather than each going their own way.

(c) The National Curriculum for 5–16-year-olds could have been planned to integrate not only with GCSE but also with the developments at 16–19 years old.

(d) It would have been possible to have worked with teachers rather than against them, giving them partial ownership of the curriculum and assessment procedures.

The Way Forward Now?

It is important that teachers are now given every possible opportunity of making the existing curriculum structure work, even if it is a less than perfect model. Changes should be made only to remove intolerable bureaucratic burdens or to put right innovations which are professionally unacceptable. The major example of that kind is that test results should no longer be used to compare LEAs, schools and teachers themselves. Comparisons based on raw scores, regardless of the standards of the pupils in the first place, are clearly misleading and unfair. In the long run there would be advantages in separating the two functions of assessment by returning to APU Testing (on the basis of light sampling, *not* every child) to monitor standards, and use National Curriculum Assessment for formative and diagnostic purposes.

Conclusion

The lesson which emerges from the 1988 National Curriculum is that educational planning – and in particular curriculum planning – should not be attempted with political timetables. There will always be occasions when politicians spot a problem and are tempted to seek a 'quick fix'. They should be strongly advised against such temptations. In education there are very few problems which lend themselves to the 'quick fix' kind of solution. Politicians should also be advised against using the National Curriculum as a way of appeasing right-wing extremists within the Conservative Party. Curriculum planners should seek consensus, not pander to ideological minority views.

6

Perspectives on the National Curriculum

Eric Bolton

In discussing the present state of the National Curriculum and how it is developing, it is important to be clear that it came into being because there were, and are, real problems in the English and Welsh Education Service which it was intended to address. Those problems mean that our compulsory schooling fails too many people, who leave school at 16 under-educated by international standards and inadequately prepared for adult working life in a complex modern society. As far back as 1978 the HMI *National Survey of Secondary Education* (DES 1978a) revealed that the curricular provision for pupils were so uneven and varied nationally as to be indefensible. Some individual pupils had very odd individual curricular programmes, and some groups of pupils experienced very unbalanced curricula. For example, most girls lost all contact with science around the age of 12 or 13 and a very large proportion of boys studied no modern languages beyond that age.

That concern about standards, and about what was actually being studied by pupils during their compulsory schooling, gave rise in 1976 to the Great Debate conducted by James Callaghan's Labour Government. Essentially, that debate sought to influence the school curriculum so that it would better meet national needs related to the economic health and well-being of the nation, and better satisfy the needs of individual pupils proceeding through their schooling. In one form or another, since that time, the debate on the school curriculum has continued. The Government of the day has become increasingly involved in that debate on the grounds that it, along with others, has an important interest in what is taught in our schools arising from its duty to the people of England and Wales as set out in the education law, and its responsibilities to foster the economic health and well-being of the nation.

Consequently, it is quite wrong to believe, or imply, that the National Curriculum of the 1988 ERA was invented out of the blue. The particular shape it took was decided by a mix of general and particular factors. But, by the time Kenneth Baker became the Secretary of State for Education, the continuing debate on the curriculum had reached the point where he either moved to legislation, or took the Government a step back from the whole business.

Not only did Government legislation for the Curriculum not come out of the blue, but it is also quite wrong to suggest that there was no coherent philosophy behind the Curriculum that emerged. From the beginning of governmental involvement in the curriculum debate the general thrust was that the curriculum for each pupil ought to be broad, balanced and relevant to their needs and to those of society and the modern world.

In addition, work on the curriculum by HMI, on its own and in co-operation with LEAs, through the 1970s and early 1980s, led to the development of a particular model of the curriculum based on areas of experience (DES 1977). That model was never intended by HMI as a curriculum itself, nor could it ever have been an operational curriculum. It was, rather, a means of planning broad, balanced and relevant curricula and a basis for analysing existing curricula.

The areas of experience were initially eight and, with the later addition of technology, became nine. The areas included the linguistic, the aesthetic, the scientific, the moral and spiritual, etc. It was always clear that translating any of those areas of experience into an actual school curriculum called for some precision in setting out what each area would consist of. Despite the rhetoric about cross-curricular themes and combined subjects such as humanities and social studies, the vast majority of secondary schools all over the country actually did deliver their curricula in terms of individual subjects.

As the curriculum debate, and the actual curriculum, developed and changed through the 1970s and early 1980s, Secretaries of State came and went. In the early 1980s Sir Keith Joseph became the Secretary of State. He was determined that standards should be high in education and that expectations and demands should be challenging and rigorous. Allied with that, he became increasingly convinced that this country should give a much better educational deal to the academically bottom 40%. In pursuit of those ends he turned his attention to the continuing curriculum debate. One of his particular contributions was to increase massively the attention paid in this country to the education services of other countries, particularly of those economic competitors closest to us culturally. Those concerns eventually persuaded Keith Joseph to give the go-ahead to the GCSE with its national subject criteria determining syllabuses and their assessment, and to produce his White Paper entitled *Better Schools* (DES 1985a).

That White Paper called for standards of achievement to be raised at every level and set out the curriculum that the Government thought all pupils ought to study during their compulsory schooling. It did so in terms almost identical with those that emerged a few years later in the 1988 ERA. The grounds on which such a curriculum was said to be needed were well rehearsed. They were grounded in the belief that there were certain areas of experience that all pupils should encounter; on notions that everybody, including the least academic pupils, should be expected to gain worthwhile qualifications, and most importantly, they were based on the belief that worthwhile curricular goals should determine what was actually assessed and how it was to be done.

By the time Kenneth Baker introduced his 1988 ERA to Parliament, the curricular debate had gone just about as far as it could without moving into actual legislation. But other things had developed as well. The Conservative Government had quite clearly decided that education, along with most other public services, needed the kind of 'hearts-and-minds' change that Mrs Thatcher was bringing to bear on British life and institutions.

Consequently, the ERA is an Act of two quite distinct and different, but related, parts. The first part is to do with the National Curriculum and its assessment. That part, as I have pointed out above, is essentially a continuation of the long-running educational and social debate about the school curriculum. The other half of the ERA has much more to do with the macro-policies of the Thatcher Government. It deals with the local management of schools (LMS), open enrolment, grant maintained schools (GMS), and the rhetoric of choice and competition, clients and consumers, and market places.

This is not the place to discuss in detail that part of the ERA, suffice it to say that pushing decision-making to the 'rim of the wheel', in other words to the school level and allowing schools to choose how to spend their money and determine their priorities for action, depends on a national curriculum being in place. This is because it enables the Government to satisfy its duties under the ERA by insisting that all schools follow the National Curriculum, and calling them to account in relation to that Curriculum through a national system of assessment. Beyond that, schools can be free, within the limits of their income and the law, to do things in whichever way they think best.

As for the National Curriculum itself, once the Government decided to move into legislation, quite regardless of its political nature and views, it had a particular problem to face: the drafting of legislation, because it is to become law, needs to be as commonly understood and as unambiguous as possible. This requirement calls for precision and specificity in the drafting of the Bill. Consequently, even if the areas of experience, or indeed any other sort of description of a school curriculum, had been possible in practice, they would create severe difficulties for the Parliamentary draftsmen when setting out the legislation. It is possible to be clear about what is commonly meant and understood by the terms 'mathematics' and 'history' to a degree that is not possible with terms such as 'humanities' or 'social studies'.

The ERA actually sets out which subjects are to be studied by all pupils; the levels of attainment that are to be expected, and the key stages in a child's schooling at which assessment and the reporting of the results of that assessment will take place. The law does not say anything about how a subject is to be organized; it does not insist that subjects should be taught as separate subjects, nor does the law have anything to say about the methodology, or teaching materials to be used. It is important to bear all this in mind in debating the problems of the National Curriculum and not to lose sight of precisely what is in the law and what is not. The ERA actually rules out any interference by Secretary of State into how things are taught and which teaching materials should be used. It is important, therefore, not to confuse what the statute has to say about what must be present, with questions of the delivery of the curriculum.

The evidence is that combined courses at secondary level and thematic, topic work in primary schools, rather than suffering, are both benefiting from the precision of the National Curriculum statute. Rather than being made impossible by the statute, such combined and thematic courses are able to ensure more effectively than previously, that the things they are said to cover are in fact dealt with. They are able to do that because the programmes of study in the statute, as distinct from the attainment targets, facilitate and enable curriculum planning. They do not dictate a specific way of organizing and carrying out the teaching and delivery of a curriculum.

By and large the National Curriculum is working out fairly well. It has its problems, of course, but the cutting edge of the work in the primary school has not run into great difficulties arising from the attainment targets and programmes of study, subject by subject. There are some difficulties, and there will be problems of overload in the primary school when all National Curriculum subjects come on stream. There are also some particular difficulties in aligning National Curriculum levels with those of the GCSE at 16-plus.

Those issues will be resolved in due course, wisely or not, as we will see. However, the really difficult and contentious issue is assessment and the reporting of its outcomes. The debate about assessment at its most honourable is of necessity one about, on the one hand, the validity or reliability of the assessments carried out, and on the other, the manageability of conducting the assessments in the classrooms and schools.

All assessment needs to come to some sort of compromise between those two demands and the assessment of the National Curriculum is no exception. Teachers understandably press for a more manageable and sensible assessment. Outside forces, however – particularly it seems national politicians – press for more validity. The snag is that in the present climate the validity question is seen by many of our politicians as only satisfactorily resolvable via a large increase in tests, wholly externally set and marked.

Many teachers and observers of the scene find it a worrying emphasis that seriously questions and undermines the place of teacher assessment in the system. However, it has its attractions to many of those teachers that have undergone some of the complex, school-based assessment that has characterized the early stages of developing the national assessment system. Consequently, there is a risk of an unholy alliance between, on the one hand, those pressing for everything to be tested by external pencil-and-paper tests and, on the other, those teachers who have found some of the assessment they have had to carry out in their classrooms so unwieldy and demanding as to be unmanageable. Many of these teachers are attracted by the call for simpler tests because, whatever may be said against pencil-and-paper tests, it cannot be said that they are difficult to organize and manage, nor that they take up excessive and undue amounts of time. Their dangerous attraction is their simplicity and speed of execution.

There are, of course, things that are best assessed via pencil-and-paper tests, but there are serious concerns about such testing becoming universal. The most serious of those is that what is tested and assessed always comes to be regarded as more important than what is not. Furthermore, if the testing itself is confined to only that which is conducive to pencil-and-paper tests, and those tests are of factual knowledge only, the backwash onto the actual business of teaching and learning in classrooms will be disastrous.

Were that to happen, the goal that Keith Joseph set the education service and the country, namely that of devising and agreeing worthwhile, challenging curricular goals for all pupils and rigorously assessing them, will have been lost. In effect, what will have happened will be that the assessment cart will have been put before the curriculum horse. If anyone wishes to see just how disastrous that can be for curricular coherence and continuity, the education of individuals and the health and well-being of the nation, they need look no further than the American school system's experience of test-led curricula.

7

The Structure for Assessment and Recording

Caroline Gipps

Introduction

The ERA of 1988 brought about wide ranging changes in education in England and Wales. Comparable changes were introduced in Scotland and Northern Ireland, which have separate educational systems. A major strand of this reform was the implementation of a National Curriculum and national assessment programme. The Conservative Government under Margaret Thatcher intended fundamentally to restructure the education system and improve the quality and availability of appropriate education in order to help overcome Britain's economic problems.

At the heart of these developments was a concern about educational standards in terms of the range of curriculum experiences offered to pupils in different schools, the rigour of teaching in the basic skills, and low expectations for pupil performance. Both the first and last of these three had been a regularly voiced criticism by the independent HMI in England and Wales.

For each subject the curriculum is enshrined in law: statutory Orders describe the matters, skills and processes to be taught as programmes of study and the knowledge, skills and understanding as attainment targets (AT) which pupils are expected to have reached at certain stages of schooling. The stages are defined as Key Stage 1 (5–7), 2 (7–11), 3 (11–14) and 4 (14–16).

The attainment targets are articulated at a series of 10 levels. The series of levels is designed to enable progression: most pupils of 7-plus are expected to be at Level 2 in the system while most pupils of 11-plus are predicted to be at Level 4 and so on. The ATs are articulated at each of the 10 levels by a series of criteria or statements of attainment which form the basic structure of a criterion-referenced assessment system.

The underlying model of the National Curriculum and assessment is

Copyright © 1993, Caroline Gipps.

therefore an objectives model of the curriculum (embodied in the attainment targets and statements of attainment) with an encouragement for teachers to focus on skills and processes (the programmes of study) linked to a criterion-referenced assessment system.

The Structure for Assessment and Reporting

The national assessment programme, as outlined in the Report of the TGAT (DES 1988) and the statutory Orders, requires that pupils be assessed against the ATs by their teachers and by external tests (called standard assessment tasks or SATs) at the ages of 7, 11, 14 and 16. At these ages the results of ATs are combined and must be reported towards the end of that school year. The results of individual pupils are confidential to themselves, their parents and teachers; results for a class as a whole and a school as a whole are to be available to the parents; results at school level are to be publicly reported at 11, 14 and 16; publication of results at 7 is not mandatory but is strongly encouraged by the Secretary of State. The publication of results is to be part of a broader report by the school of its work as a whole; the TGAT report suggested that such reports should include a general report for the area 'to indicate the nature of socio-economic and other influences which are known to affect schools'. This, however, has been ruled out by the Secretary of State. At 16 the external test is to be taken by approximately 85% of the age group, and the grading system of the GCSE is to be merged with the 10-level National Curriculum scale.

At the individual level, results must be reported to parents according to the Regulations described in Circular 5/92 (DES 1992c). This is to allow implementation of the Parents' Charter and requires all schools to report annually on all children in relation to every National Curriculum subject, including comments on general progress and a record of attendance. At the end of Key Stages the pupil's performance is to be reported in terms of levels (including at 7 years old separate arithmetic, spelling and reading levels) and comparative information is to be given about all the other pupils of the same age/stage. This comparative information of course makes the production of local league tables easy, even at age 7.

Reporting on school performance (DES 1992e) is structured specifically to allow comparative tables of school performance in public examination results at 15 and 17 (which are to be distributed by primary and middle schools to parents of children about to transfer to secondary school and published by DFE in local newspapers). Full examination results at school level should be available at least 2 weeks before choice of secondary school has to be made. Average figures for the whole of England will be supplied to Governors to go in school prospectuses.

The first run of assessment for 7-year-olds in English, maths and science took place in 1991, the first statutory run for 14-year-olds will be in 1993, for 11-

year-olds in 1994 and in that year also GCSE will be reported in line with attainment targets and National Curriculum levels. Subjects beyond the core will come on-stream and be assessed in later years, with technology being the first (1992 for 7-year-olds using a non-statutory SAT, 1993 for 14-year-olds, 1994 for 11-year-olds and 1995 for 16-year-olds). All subjects should be included in the assessment programme at all ages by 1997, though teacher assessment is likely to dominate beyond the core subjects, in conjunction with non-statutory SATs.

While the overall plan for national assessment is the same for all four ages, there are differences in articulation: national assessment at 16 is dominated by the demands of GCSE; the assessments for 11-year-olds are as yet at the blueprint stage; the 14-year-old assessments were tried in 1991, changed dramatically and then piloted in 1992; it is the assessment of 7-year-olds which is furthest along the path of development. The detailed account of the national assessment programme which follows is therefore based largely on the developments thus far in the assessment of 7-year-olds. The issues which are raised are, however, relevant to the whole programme.

During the spring and early summer term of the year in which pupils reach the age of 7 (Year 2) teachers make an assessment of each pupil's attainment on levels 1–4 of the scale 1–10 in relation to the attainment targets of the core subjects. Teachers may make these assessments in any way they wish, but observation, regular informal assessment and keeping examples of work are all encouraged. In the first half of the summer term and the second half of the spring term the pupils are given, by their teacher, a series of SATs covering a sample of the core attainment targets.

Because of the reliance on teacher assessment, the TGAT report suggested a complex process of group moderation through which teachers' assessments (TA) could be brought into line around a common standard. The combination of TA and SAT results has been a contentious area; the ruling now is that where an attainment target is assessed by both TA and SAT and the results differ, the SAT result is to be 'preferred'. If the teacher does not agree with this for an individual pupil he/she may appeal, if the SAT result would alter the overall level for the profile component (a group of attainment targets).

The SATs

Since the proposals for the SATs in the TGAT report were innovatory and were a conscious attempt to move away from traditional standardized procedures they will be described in some detail. The TGAT report suggested that a mixture of instruments, including tests, practical tasks and observations, be used in order to minimize curriculum distortion and that a broad range of assessment instruments sampling a broad range of attainment targets would discourage the narrowing tendency to teach to the test. Thus the TGAT model

was one which emphasized a wide range of assessment tasks involving a wide range of response modes, in order to minimize the negative effects normally associated with formal assessment, and within a range of different contexts to ensure content and task validity.

Early on in the development of the SATs for Key Stage 1 the requirement was that they should cover as many ATs as possible. This proved unwieldy since there are thirty-two ATs in the original curriculum structure for the core and the mode of assessment was to be active rather than pencil-and-paper tests of the traditional standardized type.

In the event, the SATs used with 7-year-olds in 1991 were a watered-down version of the TGAT proposals. They were differentiated, there was no choice of SAT task *within* attainment targets, although there was a constrained choice across ATs for science and maths. The style of assessment was, however, active and largely similar to good infant school practice: e.g. the reading task at Level 2 involved reading aloud a short passage from a children's book chosen from a list of popular titles, using dice to play maths 'games', using objects to sort, etc.

As for standardization in administration of the SATs the most important consideration is that pupils should understand what is expected of them. Thus there is no restriction on what is said or on the use of the skills of another adult who is normally present in the classroom. There is no restriction on non-linguistic methods of presentation, there is no limit on pupils working in whatever language or combination of languages they normally use in mathematics or science. However, pupils are not allowed to explain tasks to each other nor may children whose mother tongue is not English have the English tasks explained to them in their mother tongue. In effect the task administration is *not* standardized and this raises problems of interpretation.

Despite the reduction in the number of ATs tested from 32 to nine the Key Stage 1 SAT administration in 1991 took a minimum of 40 hours for a class of 25–30 and was rarely managed without support for the class teacher, since most of the SATs were done with groups of four pupils. The SATs can thus be seen as matching good teaching practice, providing teachers with detailed information about individual children, but being time-consuming and offering limited standardization for comparability purposes.

In response to the widespread publicity about the amount of time the 7-year-old SATs were taking, the Prime Minister announced in the summer of 1991 that for 1992 there would be shorter standardized paper-and-pencil tests. Similarly, the trialling of SATs for 14-year-olds which took place in 1991 involved extended tasks making many hours of classroom time and covering a range of activities and response modes. The Secretary of State for Education deemed this inappropriate and the pilot 'SATs' in 1992 were short written tests done by whole classes at the same time under examination conditions. Practical tests were only set where there was no alternative. The tests for 11-year-olds are now likely to follow the model of the 14-year-old assessments rather than the

SATs envisaged in the TGAT report.

Thus attempts to move towards a new, broader model of assessment within national assessment have been thwarted.

Discussion

Recent trends in assessment generally towards open-ended performance-based forms of assessment are now being reversed: the Government is not in favour of coursework assessment, time-consuming SATs, or teacher assessment dominating at certificating or reporting stages. The move is therefore back towards traditional examination procedures and paper-and-pencil exercises with all that this will mean for classroom practice. That said, traditional examination procedures in the UK are not of the multiple-choice type but do allow for some assessment of extended essay writing and higher order thinking skills.

The feasibility, and effect, of working to a defined progression of teaching and learning, with its underlying concept of linear progression which is at odds with constructivist models of learning, has yet to be judged. The effect of having high status external assessment in only the core can be predicted, yet the fact that the rest of the Curriculum is legislated may soften the effect.

We are seeing, however, a significant reversal of the move towards an educational model of assessment and it is important to ask why this has happened. It is partly political: assessment is being used by this administration, as in other countries, to gear up the education system, to raise standards and to force accountability on schools. In this climate, teachers are not to be trusted as their own evaluators. Neither are 'elaborate, time-consuming' assessment tasks proposed by TGAT considered appropriate. The formal, unseen examination has served the system well in the past, so the argument goes, and will do so again. It is seen as more objective, reliable and cheaper.

However, a major problem lies in the TGAT model itself. In the TGAT report there was little mention of standards and how these could be raised by testing, and limited emphasis on accountability procedures. The tone of the report was thus at odds with the political climate within which National Curriculum and assessment was introduced. Small wonder then that, as teachers complained of the workload involved in SATs and the low level of standardization became clear, the Prime Minister said the SATs would be largely paper-and-pencil tests, standardized, and capable of being taken by the whole class at once.

In addition, the model of assessment (based as it was on teacher assessment emphasizing formative and diagnostic purposes, with a range of types of task and response mode) is essentially one that is not suited to surveying the performance of *every* pupil of a particular age group at a certain point in time, particularly given the complex structure of the National Curriculum to

which it is linked. The national assessment blueprint thus did not support the administration's requirements. Add to that the apparent lowering of standards in GCSE, as an increasing proportion of the age group gained Grades A to C, and the administration clearly felt that it was time to call a halt to these particular educational developments.

The authors of the TGAT report maintain that their plan has been misinterpreted, hence the problems; but there are, nevertheless, major technical problems inherent in the blueprint (see Gipps 1992). And to suggest that summative assessment could wait until 16 when reporting was required at all four ages was naive, to say the least. What is almost more surprising is that the TGAT report was accepted in the first place, given the political agenda.

The model of assessment articulated by TGAT is one which emphasizes professional, detailed, formative assessment by teachers. For information on the performance of schools and classes different approaches are required. Testing using quicker, more reliable instruments is one way; sample surveying using more complex instruments is another; regular inspections and reports on schools will also provide the community with information about how well schools are doing, particularly at primary level where the introduction of certificating procedures is seen as less appropriate; at secondary level public examination results can be used in relation to progress scores of students, i.e. the 'value added' by the school.

The notion that one programme of assessment could fulfil four functions (formative, diagnostic, summative and evaluative) has been shown to be false: different purposes require different models of assessment (and different relationships between teacher and pupil). It may be possible to design one assessment system which measures performance for accountability and selection purposes whilst at the same time supporting the teaching/learning process, but we have not yet been able to do so.

There are three lessons to be learnt from these developments: good quality assessment is time-consuming and requires commitment; the two general functions of assessment are difficult to reconcile; assessment frameworks which do not support the aims of a powerful administration are unlikely to survive.

The Scottish experience is particularly pertinent here: the Government does not have a strong base in Scotland; teachers are better organized professionally than in England; parents have stronger educational rights. The result is that the role of external tests has changed from checking on teachers' assessments to supporting them. Add to this the absence of any requirement to publish school results to enable comparison and the Scottish model can be seen as weaker on the accountability side and stronger on the professional side. This is in direct contrast to the direction of developments in the rest of the UK.

The difference between the educational body and the political body is not just one of ideology, but also of power. It is however the case that enforced change does not always wipe out previous practice. There have been sufficient developments in England and Wales involving good practice in assessment, with teachers who have been involved in them convinced of their educational value, that it may be possible for these techniques, approaches and attitudes to survive the return to narrow testing practice with all that this will mean for teaching and learning.

8

The Shifting Scenery of the National Curriculum

Paul Black

A Sweeping and Hurried Change

The National Curriculum and national assessment constitute a vast experiment. The entire schooling in our 25,000 schools for almost all children from ages 5 to 16 is to be subject to radically new procedures. No other country in the world has a system which gives such comprehensive control to its government over the curriculum with such a frequent and closely controlled system of national assessment. Thus, there are no precedents for our new system. There are ample reasons to be fearful about the way in which these sweeping powers may be exercised.

Yet the implementation of the system is being put through with great speed, so that within 4 years of the passing of the ERA, most of its important features are in place. Thus, there has been no time for extensive trial of the new ideas. If this were a new drug, its application, even for those in dire need, would not be allowed with this degree of untried novelty.

This might all be justified if our education had been in a state of collapse before 1988. It clearly had some serious problems, but were they so bad that the only option for improvement was such an urgent and sweeping set of changes? Between 1970–1971 and 1989–1990 the percentage of pupils obtaining no graded examination results as school leavers fell from 44% to 8.3% (due in part to the raising of the school-leaving age), whilst the percentage gaining five or more higher grades at GCSE or the older equivalents rose from 7.1% to 11.4% (DES 1992d). This hardly sounds like a story of dire failure.

The changes might be defended if they were to be accompanied by thorough and independent evaluation so that the programmes could be monitored and lessons learnt from the only experience that matters, that of pupils in classrooms. My own experience in the NCC was that comprehensive programmes

Copyright © 1993, Paul Black.

for monitoring were cut back by Ministers, who have retained direct control over any research or evaluation activities of that Council. All that were allowed were programmes with modest budgets aimed to explore tightly defined questions. In consequence, evidence that the reforms as a whole might contain serious flaws cannot be forthcoming.

Nevertheless, at the same time, the Orders in science and mathematics have been revised within 2 years of their original issue (DES 1989b, 1991b). An exercise to propose similar changes for technology is now under way and the threat of a revision for English now hangs in the air. Moreover, the Secretary of State has drawn up the revisions, not on the basis of a year's work from a broadly based professional body, as for the original Orders, but on the basis of a few months' work from a small and officially anonymous group of the inspectorate. However well qualified these may be, the practice of open government here, as elsewhere, is in retreat.

The Loss of Confidence

These recent changes are very alarming portents. From my own close contacts amongst teachers in science education, I was confident, until the beginning of 1991, that the reforms were generally welcomed. Teachers were very worried about the burdens that the rapid implementation of change was placing on them. However, they accepted two things. The first was that the original definition of the National Curriculum for science was educationally sound, and that the many new features that it introduced could give a big improvement in science education. The second was that greater uniformity in science education, together with sensitive methods of assessment, could lead to all pupils being better guided throughout their learning of the subject.

This has now changed. Teachers who had spent, in 1989, many hours of extra work in a total reorganization of their teaching schemes for science and who, in 1991, were just in the second year of putting these into practice, discovered that there was to be a change. The changes turned out to be very extensive, so that all of their work for planning had to be done again. At the annual conference of the Association for Science Education in January [1992], the atmosphere of anger and cynicism among teachers was evident. A system that could make changes so quickly, without regard to its effects on their work, clearly did not appreciate or care about their professional efforts. They were drawing an even more corrosive lesson – it isn't worth taking the National Curriculum too seriously any more because it'll probably be changed again in a year or two.

The rapid changes do not seem to be grounded in evidence. The limited evaluations possible during the first year of implementation for the science and mathematics and English orders, both by HMI and by the NCC, both referred to the improvements in school work and neither made out any case that the orders needed changing quickly.

The Demise of the TGAT Report

However, the aspect of change on which I wish to concentrate is national assessment. As chair of the TGAT which reported to Kenneth Baker in January 1988 (DES 1988), I have watched the reception and subsequent implementation of that group's recommendations with particular concern.

Our report to the Minister was published very speedily. Margaret Thatcher's views were published very quickly afterwards, her concerns being revealed by way of a leak to the Opposition spokesman on education. During the next few months, both I and most other members of the task group gave a large number of talks, to the annual conferences of all of the many professional organizations in education, to various HMI meetings and to many local courses and conferences. We were greeted, in the press and at these meetings, with widespread approval for the recommendations. At no time was I faced with serious arguments for rejecting the main proposals, either in public print or at public meetings.

After a few months of public debate and government silence, Kenneth Baker made an announcement in the House of Commons broadly accepting the TGAT recommendations. The 1989 DES booklet, *From Policy to Practice* (DES 1989a), reported his commitment and set out a three page account of the main elements of the national assessment system.

Satisfaction at this outcome has been slowly but surely corroded. It is clear that most of the undertakings given in 1989 have by now, 3 years and three Secretaries of State later, been abandoned. I propose to deal with three questions that arise from this outcome. What has happened? Does it matter? How did it happen?

What Has Happened?

This is a story of death by a thousand cuts. It would be tedious to describe all the changes in detail. I shall summarize the main points in numbered order as follows – the quotations in italics are from the DES document (1989a).

(1) *'Teachers' own assessments are an essential part of the system'*. The proportion of the resources of the Schools Examination and Assessment Council (SEAC) devoted to researching and developing teachers' formative assessment has been tiny. The DES document in 1989 referred to the good practice on teacher assessment 'developed in recent years in the GCSE'. But we know by now that this good practice is no longer trusted in the way that it used to be.

(2) *'. . . pupils' achievements will not be displayed against each attainment target but the report will show the level they are at in terms of the overall profile component'*. SEAC subsequently declared that pupils' results would have to be reported against every separate attainment target. The Secretary of

State had by then put through Orders with 17 targets in science and 14 in mathematics. It seemed absurd to me that SEAC could contemplate reporting separately on such a large number, but it was not until the Examining Groups pointed out that they could not possibly do this at GCSE level with any respectable degree of accuracy that the absurdity was accepted. So the Orders for science and mathematics had to be revised to cut these numbers down.

Yet this problem should have been foreseen. In 1987/88, the Education Reform Bill was being put through Parliament by a ministerial team and their advisers who were at the same time monitoring the progress of the groups working to specify these large numbers of targets for science and mathematics. The need for a small number was never mentioned, and the Minister put the large number versions through after the Act had been finally passed. It is not possible to say who was responsible for this expensive confusion, but it is clear that thousands of science teachers, and especially the most dedicated, have, through the disruption from the later changes, suffered as a result.

(3) *'Assessment should be by a combination of national external tests and assessment by teachers'* and, talking later about the teacher's record of pupils' progress *'. . . it may be important evidence to bring to bear in moderation discussions'*. Readers of this would assume that this was an intention to implement the TGAT recommendations, which was that the results of the two forms of assessment should be combined for every reported target. They have been cruelly misled – external tests are to be the only evidence except in the case of practical and performance attainment targets, for which teachers' assessments will be the only evidence.

(4) *'Standard assessment tasks will be designed to be a support for learning, and will be drawn up under the direction of SEAC with the classroom context very much in mind. SATs for Key Stage 1 will each test attainment in a range of foundation subjects and will be designed to be administered unobtrusively. Teachers will be able to select from a bank of SATs those which most closely fit the sort of work they have been doing with their pupils'*. Such an approach was developed to the stage of extensive trials in primary schools. Some teachers complained about the workload, and, as complainants do, received more attention from the media than those who found them both challenging and helpful to their teaching practices. There was no public complaint when the Key Stage 3 trials were carried out to test the same principles. However, Kenneth Clarke quickly declared the new tests to be unacceptable and laid down new principles.

Of the new Key Stage 1 tests, an editorial in *Child Education* for last August (1992) said 'Although the tests were simplified, teachers still found them time consuming and disruptive, while in the name of manageability they had sacrificed the more interesting and worthwhile activities'. Those developing the Key Stage 3 science SATs for 1991 had asked all teachers involved to fill in feedback questionnaires about the proposed assessments and to give their opinions about various changes that could be made. The new principles embody changes to which teachers were opposed, and have abandoned many elements which commanded widespread support from teachers.

In setting out this summary, I have not used the TGAT report, but the Government's own publicity commitments, as the point of reference. I do this because the point to be underlined is not that TGAT lost the argument. We won the argument. The chilling feature is that in the world of political pressure to which education is now subject, that was of no consequence.

Does It Matter?

It could still be argued that all of these retreats are indeed improvements won by hard evidence of the impracticability of the original proposals. I would argue to the contrary that the current ideas are based on prejudice rather than evidence and are set fair to do serious harm to children's education.

Don't change too quickly
On the basis of evidence about the original plans there is no argument. None of the retreats have been based on comprehensive evidence of practices in schools, let alone on analysis of the performances of pupils or of the opinions of teachers. Moreover, anyone who has been involved closely in curriculum innovation, as I have been, learns that the first year of implementation can provide evidence for minor adjustments but cannot give valid evidence to justify large changes except where there is a serious breakdown. The reason is simple – it is only when teachers have had the time to incorporate changes into their own classroom practice that the potential of an innovation, for good or ill, can be appraised.

There is a substantial literature on innovation and change in education, notably summarized in the writing of Michael Fullan, of the University of Toronto (Fullan and Steigelbauer 1991). One clear lesson from many studies is this: changes imposed from outside which teachers are not able to take to heart and make their own are ineffective. This is not to plead that governments should be nice to teachers and respect them – although that would be a good idea – but to point out that mere imposition from outside just does not work. A teacher is in sensitive personal contact with many individual children, and has to develop his or her role by fashioning a personal style to deal with the multiple and exhausting pressures that bear in the classroom, both inside it and from outside it. You cannot treat such a person as a robot to be reprogrammed.

'Proper tests'
I start with a quotation from Kenneth Clarke from the Westminster Lecture which he gave in June 1991 (Clarke 1991) when he was Secretary of State.

> *The British pedagogue's hostility to written examinations of any kind can be taken to ludicrous extremes. The British left believe that pencil and paper examinations impose stress on pupils and demotivates them. We have tolerated for 20 years an arrangement whereby there is no national testing or examination of any kind for most pupils until they face GCSE at the age of 16 . . . This remarkable national obsession lies behind the more vehement opposition to the recent introduction of 7-year-old testing. They were made a little too complicated and we have said we will simplify them . . . The complications themselves were largely designed in the first place in an attempt to pacify opponents who feared above all else 'paper and pencil' tests . . . This opposition to testing and examinations is largely based on a folk memory in the left about the old debate on the 11-plus and grammar schools.*

I want to spend a little time on this paragraph, because it shows several of the characteristics of the current political rhetoric.

The 'complicated' 7-year-old testing to which this extract refers was recommended by TGAT. The 'complication' was a proposal that the tests be designed as pieces of classroom activity rather like a good teaching activity. Children would take some time to become involved in the activity, but then it would be so designed that they would be required to produce some writing, some number work, some measurements and so on. Thus, in the context of the work, each child would produce evidence of his or her capacity to meet the various attainment targets of the foundation subjects. The TGAT's reasons for proposing this arose from a desire to make the 7-year-old testing valid and effective. The formal timed test is a strange occasion, and any child's performance will depend strongly on skills in writing for an ill-defined audience and in capacity to understand what this strange situation is about.

Our concern was twofold. First that such tests would not give a reliable picture of what a child could do. It is evident with adults that their performance in work may be either much stronger or much weaker than their performance in a short test or interview designed to select them for that work. Staff appraisal schemes review work performance – it would be ludicrous to suggest that these use written tests instead. If this is so for adults, how much more true must it be for 7-year-old children whose capacities to communicate and to understand the significance of what is happening to them are so much more limited? Of course capacity to write must be assessed, but if a child is strong in other areas and weak in written expression, it is misleading if the strengths are not revealed because of reliance on only one mode of communication.

Secondly, any external tests are bound to exert pressure on teaching methods; teachers will be tempted to drill pupils to perform in the tests. The aim therefore must be to make the test such that preparation and rehearsal is a good way of learning. So the assessments were designed to be models of good learning with assessment firmly built in. Since we also believed that classroom assessment by teachers was an area of weakness, it was hoped that these well-designed pieces would be models of good practice. I believe that they were and that those who complained about the work-load were actually struggling with getting hold of a more stringent model of teaching and assessment than they had been used to.

All of this reasoning was in the TGAT report. It is deeply disturbing to have it rejected because it was 'complicated' and because it was 'designed to pacify opponents who feared . . .'. I do not mind if our arguments are confronted with counter-argument and evidence, but I find it offensive to have them attacked by imputation of the motives of the group which I chaired. The imputation is in any event strange. The group included, with myself and others, people who had for many years been responsible for paper-and-pencil tests taken by hundreds of thousands of pupils in our public examination systems, in APU testing, and in the numerous standardized and diagnostic tests used by schools. We knew far more about paper-and-pencil testing than any of the right-wing critics; in particular, we were well aware of their strengths and of their weaknesses and were struggling to use that expertise to fashion an optimum system.

The second feature of the arguments in the passage is even more disturbing. Opposition and opposing arguments are lumped together. If one asks 'Who is being attacked here?', then it appears that in the first line it is 'The British pedagogue'; on the next line this becomes 'The British left'. Near the end, there is a clear reference to the TGAT group. The reasons given by some groups, which were not TGAT's reasons, are lumped together in a single linked wave of criticism. This stereotyping of all expert opinion and evidence is very common in political argument. The effect that I have noticed is that many of us who really believe in the value of tough and reliable assessment are being bracketed together with those opposed to all testing and thereby labelled as woolly-minded. I fear that critics in Government do not really understand the deep difference between those who want to break away from traditional tests in order to improve assessment and testing because they care about it, and those who want to abandon it altogether.

The result of such indiscriminate arguments will be a return to tests of poor validity, dangerous unreliability and with a heritage of damaging effects on pupils' learning. It is not clear why these traditional tests are so preferred – it appears that they bear the image of 'traditional values' in this field, that they might have the advantage that teachers who are not to be trusted are not involved in them, perhaps even that they must be good because the 'pedago-gues' and/or the 'left-wing' don't like them.

Assessment and learning

I have spent more than 2 of the last 4 months in the USA. The practice of assessment there is undergoing a rapid change. The use of short external standardized tests, almost always multiple-choice tests, has been widespread for several decades, and the technical expertise in developing these has reached a far higher level than anywhere else in the world. However, many of the States are now abandoning them, because it is evident that they have done almost nothing to improve education. Since 1989, 16 of the States have started to develop and implement alternative forms of assessment in science, 20 in mathematics, and a review, in Spring [1992], said that further new initiatives are developing rapidly (Blank and Dalkilic 1992).

Their new interest is in tests of performance, which are closer to good classroom practice, which take longer to use, and in which teachers can be fully involved. One of their chief sources of ideas in this drive to find more valid and useful forms of assessment has been Great Britain. The work of many agencies here, and particularly the reports of the APU, are well known and much used. The TGAT report is also well known. I have spoken to many of those involved in these changes. They are astonished to hear what is now happening here – they see us as marching backwards into the unprofitable ways from which they are now escaping. Ironically, one of their chief objects of admiration – the APU – was an initiative of our Government. Its lessons had a profound effect on the TGAT deliberations. They are influencing USA policies. They appear now to have little, if any, effect on our own Government's policy.

I would like to expand on this point a little more. First let me give an assurance – my reporting of trends in the USA does not derive from chats with a few academic friends. I have been invited to take part in consultations with the State Departments of Education in California and Connecticut, I have been involved, with foreign experts from other countries, to formulate policy advice for the National Science Foundation and I have worked as the only overseas invited expert on a committee of the US National Academy of Sciences charged with drawing up advice on assessment standards for a new national statement on the future science curriculum for US schools.

I can illustrate the nature of the current concerns in the USA by quoting from the most recent authoritative book on the subject, entitled *Changing Assessments: Alternative Views of Aptitude Achievement and Instruction* (Gifford and O'Connor 1992). This is a collection of studies by 12 leading authorities in the USA produced under the aegis of their National Commission on Testing and Public Policy and published earlier this year.

Here, first of all are three quotations from a closing summary by Professor Lorrie Shepard:

> *The most important contribution . . . is the insight that all learning involves thinking. It is incorrect to believe, according to old learning theory, that the basics can be taught by rote followed by thinking and reasoning. As documented by the Resnicks, even comprehension of simple texts requires a process of inferring and thinking about what*

the text means. Children who are drilled in number facts, algorithms, decoding skills or vocabulary lists without developing a basic conceptual model or seeing the meaning of what they are doing have a very difficult time retaining information (because all the bits are disconnected) and are unable to apply what they have memorised (because it makes no sense).

'Measurement-driven instruction' will lead reform in the wrong direction if tests embody incomplete or low-level learning goals.

Various efforts to reform assessment use terms such as 'authentic', 'direct' and 'performance' assessment to convey the idea that assessments must capture real learning activities if they are to avoid distorting instruction.

(Shepard 1992)

The article by Resnick and Resnick, to which Shepard refers, develops a critique of the multiple-choice or very short answer tests which were until recently almost the only form of testing in USA schools:

Children who practice reading mainly in the form in which it appears in the tests – and there is good evidence that this is what happens in many classrooms – would have little exposure to the demands and reasoning possibilities of the thinking curriculum.

Students who practised mathematics in the form found in the standardized tests would never be exposed to the kind of mathematical thinking sought by all who are concerned with reforming mathematical education . . .

(Resnick and Resnick 1992)

The article goes on to emphasize the inevitable effects on reaching of any tests designed for accountability purposes, and concludes:

Assessments must be so designed that when you do the natural thing – that is, prepare the students to perform well – they will exercise the kinds of abilities and develop the kinds of skills that are the real goals of educational reform.

(Resnick and Resnick 1992)

The article then describes assessments which would have a positive effect on teaching. Of the three examples given, one is the teacher-assessed project in the former Joint Matriculation Board (JMB) Engineering Science and a second was a test of higher order thinking skills devised by the US National Assessment of Educational Progress (NAEP) which drew heavily on APU science items and for which one of my APU science team was a consultant. The authors conclude that:

If widely adopted as part of the public accountability assessment system, performance assessments (including portfolio assessments) could not only remove current pressures for teaching isolated collections of facts and skills but also provide a positive stimulus for introducing more extending thinking and reasoning activities in the curriculum.

(Resnick and Resnick 1992)

Finally, another quotation from Shepard which could have been written as a commentary on the current position in this country:

If they are unaware of new research findings about how children learn, policy makers are apt to rely on their own implicit theories which were most probably shaped by the theories that were current when they themselves attended school ... Some things that psychologists can prove today even contradict the popular wisdom of several decades ago. Therefore, if policy makers proceed to implement outmoded theories or tests based on old theories, they might actually subvert their intended goal – of providing a rigorous and high quality education for all students.

(Shepard 1992)

Assessment in the classroom

I do not agree with all of the arguments of the Resnicks in the work quoted above. They want to emphasize the difference between external accountability tests and teachers' own assessments. However, their arguments are in all other respects very close to the TGAT arguments. They emphasize the need to develop teachers' formative assessment and the need for summative assessments to be as faithful to good learning practice as possible.

The point I want to emphasize here is that, because teachers know their pupils well and can assess their progress on many and varied occasions over a long time, they are in a far better position to make a more authentic and reliable assessment of a pupil's work than any external test can achieve. If such assessments are valued and play a significant part in accountability assessments, then the undesirable effects of testing on good learning can be avoided. However, a great deal needs to be invested to develop good practice in formative assessment.

It was also clear to the TGAT group that external assessments must also be used to calibrate teachers' own assessments, whilst discrepancies between the two ought to be discussed with groups of teachers by a set procedure for resolving differences in the light of evidence. Such monitoring meetings are known to be of great professional value to all involved. All of this has been rejected, and it does seem as if those rejecting do not understand the limitations of external tests and do not share the TGAT view of the prime importance of improving the practice and the status of teachers' formative assessments as essential to good teaching and learning. Another quote from Shepard reinforces the point here:

> . . . *the teacher has need of constant information about what the student knows and the strategies being used to process and comprehend new concepts . . . By imbedding diagnostic instruction in instructional activities, teachers can preserve the integrity of assessment tasks (the wholeness of tasks and natural learning context) and protect instructional time that would otherwise be diverted to testing . . . There is general agreement that external packaged tests will not solve the problem of what teachers need to know about student learning.*

> (Shepard 1992)

The APU assessments were related as closely as possible to the best classroom practice, but went ahead of it in showing how new aims could be assessed faithfully. The new assessment methods and items so developed have been welcomed and used by many teachers. Many of these new methods cannot be implemented in the short time limited external test.

The TGAT group were well aware that short, time-limited external tests are bound to emphasize isolated and disconnected pieces of knowledge. We also were concerned that such emphasis was bound to feed back into the classroom and put teachers under pressure to teach for such tests, a practice which would do damage to good learning practice. Drawing on arguments very similar to those quoted above, and on the extensive development of good assessment experiences in this country, the TGAT report tried to open up the possibility that a new positive relation between good teaching and good assessment could be developed. That prospect is now receding, and drilling for the test is now taking its place, to the dismay of many teachers and the potential impoverishment of many pupils.

Can the results be trusted?

The reliability of tests which are used to judge schools and to influence the future of pupils must clearly be a matter of great concern. To take an example, at Key Stage 3 pupils' national assessment in three of the four attainment targets in science will be settled by a single 3-hour test, externally set and written as a formal timed examination. The test has to produce results separately on each of the three targets, which gives 1 hour per target. The question at issue is – can such a short test produce an answer that can be trusted?

In the APU work, considerable effort was devoted to finding out how reliable the survey results were. It was shown that if a pupil was set two different sets of questions designed to test the same thing, the results could be very different. To choose either one of them to label that pupil would be unfair because of the inaccuracy. The average of the two, or better still, the results of tests using more questions, could give a better estimate. The technical results of such studies have been published by the DES itself (DES 1988). There is nothing new about such results – everyone knows that examination results can be inaccurate, and when pupils could take the same subject with two different GCE boards, reports of wide differences in some of the results were commonplace.

It is also clear that the shorter the test, the less reliable its result can be. From all the evidence that I know from my involvement in the APU science work, the result of 1 hour of testing on science performance in an attainment target will be untrustworthy. To cover the ground, the test will be bound to adopt those narrow forms of test items which the USA State authorities are abandoning after decades of experience with them.

Data on the reliability of the 1990 and 1991 pilots and trials of the SATs have not been published, and the new versions, being shorter in time, will probably be less reliable. At a public presentation given last January [1992] by SEAC officers about these new science tests I asked what studies would be undertaken to determine how reliable the new tests will be. I was told that there would be none. I asked whether that meant that there would be no data available to the public about how reliable the test results will be. I was told that in my sense of the word reliability, that was so. The sense in which I was asking about reliability was about whether a pupil taking an identical test, or a similar test, such as, for example, might be set for the SAT next year, would be likely or not to get the same result on both tests. Clearly, if the chances for this are low, the test result will be worthless and teachers, pupils and parents will be well advised to ignore the results.

How Did It Happen?

I am not able to give more than a few indications to answer this question. We could all do so if the changes that have occurred to the policy announced in 'From Policy to Practice' had happened as an outcome of reasoned public debate, but that has not been the case. We could do so if evidence to support the new strategies had been quoted and could be examined. There has been little evidence, but many broad assertions.

Eric Bolton (1992) has drawn attention to the overwhelming influence, on current Government policy in education, of the right-wing pressure groups, notably the Centre for Policy Studies. One of its leading figures replaced the dismissed chairman of SEAC. It is now clear that the changes to the memberships of the NCC and assessment council give each of these an increasing bias towards that particular element in our governing party. Because of this, the teaching profession is rapidly losing any serious respect for these councils.

The hopes of many that the Government would exercise their sole power to appoint to the councils in an impartial way have been sharply disappointed. Those who gave dire warnings that the ERA would be an instrument for direct

Government control in which the opinions of ministers would be insulated from professional opinion and expertise have been proved correct.

Of course, it may be that the bulk of that opinion and expertise is deeply in error. In the pressure groups' rhetoric, the so-called educational establishment has been elevated to the status of bogeyman, and the terms 'expert', 'academic', 'researcher' have been turned into terms of abuse. As an expert academic researcher who saw the Act as a force for good, and who has given much of his time to trying to help its development, I am deeply disappointed and fearful at the outcomes I have described in this paper.

However, if it is true that the judgements and experience of the whole so-called 'educational establishment' have to be dismissed, then we really are in very profound trouble. If the teaching profession's practices and judgements are no longer to be trusted, then the fault cannot be corrected simply by giving them new orders. They are not robots. All who care for education should not want them to be robots. To treat them as if they were robots is to run the risk that they will start to behave as robots.

Note

This paper is the Presidential Address to the Education Section of the British Association Science Festival '92, delivered at the University of Southampton, 25 August 1992.

9

Values, National Curriculum and Diversity in British Society

Jagdish Gundara

Peter Newsam (1988) has stated that the National Curriculum entitles all children to 'a common set of educational experiences pitched at a high level'. If such entitlements and experiences are to become a reality they cannot take place when schools are part of a market with losers and winners. The value of a common national curriculum for all children in a diverse and unequal society could be to facilitate equalities of outcomes if the curriculum is negotiated in comprehensive schools. As Brian Simon states:

> If we genuinely wish to offer a full entitlement curriculum, or set of common educational experiences at all, this requires, at least at the current historical stage, the full and deliberate implementation of comprehensive education – and in every area of the country.
>
> (Simon 1992, p. 82)

Entitlement becomes less real if one set of children attends schools which are outside the comprehensive system. The logistics of ensuring entitlement even within the state system are difficult if suitable teachers and material resources are not made available. A central aspect of the 'common experience' is the common and shared learnings and understandings that children and teachers can develop by critically negotiating the curriculum. This chapter explores the issues that schools need to address in such a negotiated curriculum and the legal, societal and political constraints that stand in their way.

Accountability and Partnership in a Diverse Society

In order to deliver the National Curriculum and ensure its assessment, the Government is setting up the School Curriculum and Assessment Authority. The Authority and the Office of Her Majesty's Chief Inspector of Schools will be 'central pillars of our educational architecture' (DES 1992f, p. 9). Both of these are required to bring coherence and quality into the curriculum and assessment arrangements.

Under the new arrangements, schools acquire accountability both to these central bodies and locally to parents. This accountability amounts to a very narrow definition of the school as an institution within the public domain. The partnership between the teachers, parents and pupils excludes the wider social, communal and public context in which schools are located. This is reinforced by the Parents' Charter with its emphasis on parental choice, test results and market principles.

In a strong education system, the partnership between schools and their communities should enable them to deal with the value dilemmas within our society. The learning process takes place not only in the classroom but also in the playground where more complex values and identities of the locality permeate the school (Cohen 1991). It is only through the wider partnership of the school and diverse communities that a common civic culture to which all children subscribe can develop. Such a shared civic culture, drawing on the strengths of a diverse society, could assist the growth of a genuinely participatory democracy.

The National Curriculum should reflect this broadly based diversity in British society. If the Curriculum is to involve the various cultures and civilizations which are part of the British body politic, then there is a great merit in its classroom negotiation.

The Substance of Entitlement

The stress on entitlement implicit in the National Curriculum has rightly been seen as a genuine advance. Yet if this legal entitlement is to become a reality, all children in Britain ought to have access to a common curriculum based on universal principles. Entitlement to an ethnocentric English curriculum does not constitute such an entitlement. A narrowly defined curriculum can be based on fantasizing or on ideological construction of the 'Others'' past. In fact, the construction of such a curriculum assumes that there is a monocultural future. Such an assumption is a fallacy because a multicultural future is already with us; the denial of it presents pupils with distorted values and endangers the polity. A previous Secretary of State stated that pupils from African, Caribbean and Asian backgrounds ought to be taught Western classical music. What the Secretary of State ignored was that it is equally incumbent upon an English child to understand and enjoy icons of Oriental and African classical traditions. This is particularly the case because contemporary youth culture is influenced by music from a very diverse range of backgrounds.

Can a National Curriculum ignore this important issue and impose a narrow English understanding of what is falsely constructed as a Western tradition? As Martin Bernal (1987) points out, Ancient Greece (the parent of Europe) acquired vast learning from the Egyptian and Phoenician civilizations (see also Gundara 1990). Culture is a socially plural construction which is not dissimilar from Bakhtin's (1981) conception of language as a socially plural construct in which our own speech is never entirely exclusively our own, but always heteroglossic and polyvocal. Culture and language are at the borderline between oneself and the other. As Clifford (1984, p. 237) states, the word in language is 'half someone else's': it is never all one's own. In defining the National Curriculum it is important to avoid dominant monologues and establish dialogues which would give a stake to all in the negotiated curriculum. In developing the oral and written skills of students in English language, the Working Party Report pointed out the importance of building on the students' own linguistic experiences and skills. The English curriculum can assist students in developing a critical edge to their thinking.

The rationale for establishing such a commitment within the National Curriculum is not merely to demonstrate tolerance to diversity, but more to overcome the dichotomy between 'them' and 'us'. An approach to the curriculum on this basis presents immense challenges for the institutional pedagogies and curriculum within schools as well as for teacher education. An inclusive perspective in the National Curriculum would provide a sounder basis for building upon the diverse values within British society, and have implications for all social interactions.

The history curriculum in particular, represents a site for questioning local communities and British society. Issues of societal diversity and migration can help students to enlarge their understanding of the complexity of the underlying society and enable them to re-interpret history and make connections. British history therefore cannot be taught merely as a story of England. Moving from the more immediate 'family and adults around them' at Key Stage 1 to other statutory Core Study Units in other Key Stages, students are required by the National Curriculum to engage with perspectives of European explorers as well as of indigenous peoples in parts of the world which were explored, exploited and settled. Making these connections is important because it allows students to understand the underlying complexity of most human societies.

Educational initiatives which lead to making diversities cohere are important in a period of fragmentation. A curriculum which de-emphasizes racism and narrow ethnicisms can nurture and assist the development of healthily rooted but dynamic common cultures. Students and teachers ought to be enabled to negotiate critically core values to which all can subscribe and which result from a broader understanding of the commonalities in a socially diverse society.

From this perspective, the shift is not towards a mindless cosmopolitanism (Koupat 1992, pp. 232–248). It is, in fact, a constructive engagement with progressive specificities and particularities of diverse cultural groups, without the parochialism which is bound to grow if exclusion, racism and ethnicization of cultures continue. A recognition, for instance, of 'Englishness' would entail an understanding of its symbiotic relationship with the more complex and larger aspects of 'Britishness'. As such, this ought not to be seen as the English liberal tradition, writ large as universal, but a genuine attempt to engage with the complex diversities of all groups within British society.

A curricular development which engages with such questions presents teachers and pupils with a very large canvas, involving the possibility of genuine negotiation and development both of pupils' critical faculties, and of teachers as professionals. Such critical engagement would challenge old certainties and self-evident truths. It entails a disengagement from the moralisms which emanate from various quarters, including the privileging notions of 'sovereign unitariness' or superficial 'celebration of diversity'. The National Union of Teachers also stresses the development of whole school policies to establish a climate for positive learning where all feel equally valued. Such policies need to cover all aspects of school life; they need to involve everyone so that they feel 'ownership' of the policy, school ethos, effects of school organization, links with parents and community, curriculum both formal and hidden, assessment, religious education and worship, language policy, staffing issues dealing with racist incidents, monitoring and circulation (NUT 1992, p. 3).

A critical reading of all messages, particularly the visual ones, which pervade contemporary culture, merits curriculum development work. This needs to happen without further undermining progressive local, regional and national values. Are there ways in which curriculum developments in English and media studies can engage with these values and relate them to those which are universal? In the absence of such developments, jingoism and regressive nationalism would persist unchallenged.

The central question is whether policy makers will tackle issues of values and boundaries in order to enable teachers and pupils to learn within creative spaces in schools. The implementation of the National Curriculum offers an opportunity to ensure that the dominant discourses engage creatively with those which are marginalized or subordinated. A continued assertion of the dominant mode would in turn nurture the growth of siege mentalities and disaffections within the polity. Such issues have an immediacy and cannot be considered as merely theoretical or distant, and curriculum development could have a critical function in arresting this process.

Religious Education and Secular Values in Education

As a specific example of this, we now turn to how religious education might be handled. In many states around the world the 'church' and the 'state' are divided for good reasons. In Britain the connection between the Crown and the

Anglican Church still exists, although the society is largely considered secular. The recent White Paper emphasizes spiritual and moral development and states: 'Proper regard should continue to be paid to the nation's Christian heritage and traditions in the context of both the religious education and collective worship in schools' (DES 1992f, 8.2).

It is not sufficient to treat issues of a multifaith society in this manner. The mere provision for children of other faiths to worship (i.e. withdraw) suggests that only Christianity has a recognized status. In children's minds other faiths remain second-class and exotic. This detracts from the understanding of other faiths and is in itself divisive. Such divisiveness may in turn lead to conflict, with faiths like Islam being equated with fundamentalism *per se*. Furthermore, all Asians may get constructed as 'Muslim fundamentalists' and notions of religious equality may be thrown to the winds.

At another level this privileging of Christianity raises serious issues for the multi-faith nature of British society and has implications for the secular nation state. More importantly for schools, moral values derived from Christianity or Islam are but one dimension of the more complex value dilemmas confronting the younger generation. This is particularly the case since youth and peer group values themselves are an important feature of the culture of the school.

Within the British and European context, religious conflicts during the Renaissance were conflicts between different Christian communities (between Roman Catholics and Protestants, or between different Protestant communities). These conflicts then extended to the Turks. 'Freedom of religion' meant freedom to belong or not to belong to any group which originated from the Jewish and Christian traditions. The 'non-believers' such as humanists had to fight longer to obtain the same rights as religious groups. In general terms the *de facto* separation of church and state was accepted by most groups.

It is from this perspective that fundamentalist belief systems which reject the separation of 'church' and 'state' are often seen as threatening the freedom of religion of all other groups. The notion of an Islamic city where there are no divisions between the public and the private and no civic culture poses a new challenge to the modern and secular society. Dividing the public from the private is not only a feature of a representative democratic framework, but also may be seen as leading to a creative dialectical relationship between what are essentially different but enhancing social spheres. The private domain in this context should not be seen as offering a licence from mainstream society or a sanction for alienation, withdrawal and moral aloneness. Indeed, the public, secular framework has a vital role in nurturing the viability of Islamic communities. At the same time, we broaden our understanding of the development of secular societies by embracing the learnings and understandings of other cultures.

Given religious diversity in Britain, it is necessary to arrive at clear definitions about the secular nature of this society and the rights and obligations of various citizens and groups. Recent events have led not only to antagonism towards Islam, but resentment directed at others who are not even Muslims.

This raises questions at two levels. One is how Britain ensures that within its modern secular context Muslims and others of different faith communities will receive equal treatment and freedom of speech alongside their obligations as citizens. Secondly, it includes for educators a much more serious issue: of an accretion of feelings, ways of seeing and understanding on the part of the English towards those who are classified as the 'Other' and whose voices are ignored. If religious education is to be taught, this is a major dimension of the notion of entitlement within a multifaith curriculum. The Standing Advisory Councils on Religious Education have drawn up many successful agreed syllabuses which reflect the diversity of values in local areas. However, this diversity of values cannot merely be taken to mean religious values. There are obviously within all the communities a large number of families who do not practise any religion. This poses questions not just about a religious education curriculum but about a broadly based values education. An analysis of the notion of secularism can extend our understanding of the intellectual issues educators need to confront to produce an adequate approach to values education in a diverse society.

The rise of theocracy in diverse societies in modern terms cannot be ignored. The rise, even in secular societies, of electronic churches (as in the United States) is a pointer to the type of fundamentalism which may need to be faced in considering the multifaith nature of most societies. In times of uncertainty the symbol systems of religions strike a stronger chord even amongst those who are non-believers than the diffuse systems of secularism in societies. Educators (together with social scientists) need to reappraise the nature of secular education and its role in strengthening the legitimacy of all citizens in currently narrowly-defined nation states. The exclusion of knowledge drawn from linguistic, religious, social and ethnic communities poses major challenges for all involved in education. At a societal level, fundamentalist beliefs about the market economy can have similar exclusive effects, and can give rise to fundamentalisms in other domains.

The rise of such strong belief systems in modern secular societies may be a reflection of how secular states have failed to provide a safe and secure framework for diverse faith communities. It may also be partly attributable to strong assertions of human rights which are not accompanied by effective measures to ensure their implementation, at both political and social levels. Religious and values education merits a newer sensitivity in schools and requires new knowledge and skills in teachers.

The growth of secularism has taken root after long struggles. In some quarters there is a tendency to view secularism as modern paganism and conflate it with humanism. Humanism is a philosophical system in which humanity, not divinity, is central. Secularism is largely a legal system which provides the necessary framework to nurture equality for all citizens at the public level and to safeguard the sacred at the private level.

The secular collectivity is not necessarily theistic, atheistic or agnostic. Optimally it provides a 'nest' for all age groups and protects their citizenship and rights. 'Positive secularism' (Verma 1986) or 'the nest' in this sense goes beyond religious toleration of other groups. It entails an understanding by all citizens and students of our shared belongingness in a complex society of diverse groups and values. This requires that children do not exclude certain values and groups from their mental maps.

Many secular societies are being challenged by the demand for religious schooling, or an education system based on one religion. These demands are in contradiction with the notions of 'positive secularism'. Problems arise immediately with the promotion or the dominance of one particular religion in state schools or when certain behaviour, based on religious conviction, is denied in schools (for instance the refusal in French schools to allow Muslim girls to wear head shawls). However, the issue is not whether religious education should be implemented in all secular schools for wearing a crucifix or a shawl. The issue is how to reconsider the consequences of secularism for education. Secular education as such is not neutral education, and ought to form an important dimension within the cross-curricular theme of citizenship.

The school ought to respect the moral autonomy of students. It would be failing if it did not provide the students with a critical edge to their thinking, which could in turn provide them with a solid foundation to defend their belief systems. The critical negotiation of values by teachers and students may be a greater challenge for schools than the attempts to merely transmit them. At another level this raises the issue of how to translate such understanding to living within complex social institutions, including workplaces.

Institutionalized education belongs to the public domain. This division itself is problematic in Britain and requires further thought. This is particularly so at present because the state does not promote the notion of a 'nest' in which minority groups feel safe. The division of the private and public should enhance everyone's well-being. One of its functions should be to counter the devaluing of subordinated groups. There is a problem here, since only a few religious communities have a fundamental right to establish their own schools, and these do not necessarily promote mutual interfaith understanding. More importantly, others are not permitted to do the same. This raises an important question about denominational voluntary-aided schools. Would the creation of Islamic denominational schools lead to the creation of ghetto schools? Would such schools be seen as being at the bottom of the league and make the rhetoric of equality even emptier?

Since one religion cannot dictate to a heterogeneity of religions in a secular society, a distinction between private morality and law, as well as between sin and crime, needs to be drawn. The nurturing and inculcation of a secular morality and value-system within public institutions becomes incumbent on schools. The ensuing distinction between metaphysical concerns and political ethics is important to enable an encompassing confidence in the polity as a whole.

In principle a critical negotiation of values by teachers and students should be limited to the values of the secular state within the public domain. The school in a plural society should by definition not interfere in the private and autonomous domain of the individual and the family, because the essence of pluralism is the recognition of and respect for diverse lifestyles and belief systems. However, the school as a social institution ought to enable students to understand issues pertaining to the common good of all members of the school and the society of which it is a part. The school should not ignore religious knowledge and values as they relate to public values of a diverse and secular society.

Religious instruction belongs to the private domain, but ethical, religious, spiritual and philosophical knowledge is part of the public domain and can be taught with the aim of religious tolerance, which is a prerequisite for the maintenance of democracy. This is not a single curriculum area nor one that can be taught in isolation. It must be part of the context and content of all the subjects of the curriculum, and not relegated to the personal, social element of it. To uphold the values and future of a healthy secular state in our society, religious education must be seen as part of the wider values education which informs the planning and implementation of the whole curriculum.

Atomized Values

The younger generation face greater value dilemmas because of the atomization of values within various communities. The stress on the market economy for the past decade and a half at the expense of the social policy framework of society has helped to further this. The educative functions of the mass media can be enhanced if children are enabled to read media messages and images critically and to evaluate the values transmitted by the media. The intrusion of mass media into our children's lives leads to value dilemmas, particularly over commercial values which undermine the values of the family and the vibrancy of local communities. In the context of an unequal society a focus on commercialization can lead to the destabilization of common social structures. Economic literacy and numeracy are essential so that students can understand and cope in these realms. Where the lack of such literacy has a racial dimension the problems for the schools are compounded even further. Schools therefore confront immense problems which the rhetoric of the recent White Paper does not address in the least. The Department for Education ought to read the situation from across the Atlantic with circumspection. Magnet schools and what they represent are only one side of the coin. There is at the underlying level a grave inequality, such that entitlement to the curriculum becomes merely notional (Kozol 1991, Hacker 1992). This is particularly the case where issues of special needs and bilingual pupils have resource implications and are a barrier to access to the curriculum. The difficulties of disadvantaged inner city and rural schools in providing an entitlement curriculum, in the face of the massive inability to educate, is a major issue. Geoff Whitty states:

> *The government's own insistence that such schools should teach the National Curriculum could also be seen as a cynical ploy to make it appear that there is a measure of equal treatment for all pupils when the structures that emanate from the other measures all conspire to deny it having any meaningful effect.*
>
> (Whitty 1990, p. 33)

Parents and pupils who are victims of this cynical machiavellianism are already experiencing the divisive effects of such measures. This further fracturing of civil society adds to value dilemmas already present. Yet as Whitty (1990) states (p. 34): 'The National Curriculum is there as one remaining symbol of a common education system and specifiable entitlement which people can struggle collectively to improve.'

To enable schools and teachers to undertake this task requires value issues to be negotiated in every subject and to permeate the whole curriculum. The relegation of such crucial issues to the currently marginalized courses of personal and social skills is totally insufficient. Yet, paradoxically, the Parents' Charter lays more stress on the examination-based performance of the children and devalues a well-rounded education – all at the expense of the real 'consumers' of education – the students.

Note

I would like to thank my colleagues Ms Rozina Vizram and Dr Robert Cowen for their helpful suggestions.

10

The National Curriculum and Special Education Needs

Brahm Norwich

Introduction

Recent developments in the special educational field over the last two decades have been concerned with the broad question of including those with difficulties in learning into the mainstream of education. A landmark was the introduction of those with severe intellectual difficulties into the schools system in the early 1970s. The Warnock Report (DES 1978b) consolidated much of this thinking and came to represent the integrative move. This was found not only in the principle of educating children with special educational needs (SEN) in ordinary schools, but in the very adoption of the term 'special educational needs'. By talking and thinking in this way the aim was to break down barriers between those pupils with difficulties in ordinary and those in special schools. Along with this was the principle of a common curriculum for all and modifying it in terms of individual needs. This integrative movement was central to the Warnock philosophy and was based on the underlying principle that the aims of education were the same for all children. The significance of the 1988 National Curriculum needs to be understood in this context.

I will discuss in this chapter what appears to be one of the fundamental issues concerning the National Curriculum for SEN, the tension between a common entitlement and meeting individual needs. The particular emphasis will be on how the National Curriculum applies to those pupils with significant difficulties in learning, those with Statements of special educational needs. Most of these pupils are in special schools and units, but about a third are now in ordinary schools. I recognize that there are important concerns about the wider group of those with SEN in ordinary schools. However, the applicability and relevance of the National Curriculum is best judged in relation to those with significant difficulties. The chapter will involve a discussion of some of the underlying issues, their implications for attitudes to the current National Curriculum and finally some ideas about how changes to the National Curriculum would better suit those with special educational needs.

A Fundamental Issue

In asserting that the aims of education are the same for all children, the Warnock Committee (1978) was endorsing the liberal democratic value that all children be treated as of equal value and be entitled to learn the best of what was considered worth learning. These values have been expressed in the principle of a common curriculum entitlement for all, a principle which is supported by a widespread commitment amongst educators to democratic values. In consolidating and expressing this principle the Warnock Committee paid little attention to how a common entitlement could be implemented and be made to work in practice.

The introduction of a National Curriculum which specifies a common progression of learning outcomes has brought this oversight to the fore. The breadth of the National Curriculum requirement defined in terms of subjects has made it hard for teachers to see how the balance of learning activities can be adapted to take account of exceptional needs. It has left teachers wondering how their established and successful curricula can be preserved and integrated with National Curriculum requirements. The 10-level system of attainment as the framework for National Assessment arrangements has also raised considerable concerns about the relevance of National Curriculum assessment. Optimism about inclusion in mainstream education is thus confronted with anxiety over the inflexibility of the 1988 National Curriculum. Would there be difficulties for *any* national curriculum, not just the 1988 one, in trying to encompass all pupils? My position is that any such curriculum would be faced with the challenge of establishing a worthwhile common entitlement given the diversity of individual needs. There is a fundamental tension between the two considerations. This tension between individuality and equality can be expressed as a dilemma about how to design a national common curriculum framework. The more the entitlement is specified, the less relevant and applicable it will be to those with exceptional needs; the more the entitlement is in general terms, the less likely will it apply in practice to all pupils. The dominant view of SEN since the Warnock Report has been one-sided in promoting the principle of inclusion, without recognizing the tension between inclusion and individuality. These principles can be balanced against each other, but doing so leads to some trade-off between them. I will argue that a optimal balance will depend, amongst other factors such as teaching resources, on how a common curriculum is designed. By implication, poor designs can result in a less than satisfactory balance and inadequate curricula for those with SEN.

Implementing the National Curriculum

Much has been written about the way that the original design and specific form of the 1988 National Curriculum has taken little account of children with SEN (Daniels and Ware 1990, Lewis 1991). I do not intend to repeat these comments here. I will summarize, however, what have been identified as obstacles to their full participation in these terms:

(a) the similar breadth of content across the different phases of schooling (Key Stages);
(b) the amount included in the National Curriculum;
(c) the use of a 10-level system of defining attainment levels for all areas of learning;
(d) the linking of programmes of study to Key Stage;
(e) the time required for and the few teaching benefits of the extensive use of national Standard Assessment Tasks;
(f) the relative lack of cross-curricular elements.

These and other features of the 1988 National Curriculum present difficulties for all children, not just those with SEN (cf. other contributions in this book). However, these features pose especial difficulties for those with exceptional needs, and in one sense the appropriateness of the 1988 National Curriculum for the latter is a good test of its comprehensiveness. The need for exceptions, modifications and disapplications, depends therefore on the appropriateness of the National Curriculum in the first instance. The possible use of informal exceptions for the wider group of pupils with SEN not requiring Statements, and of formal exceptions, should be evaluated in this context. This means that the more flexible and relevant a national curriculum is for those with SEN, then the less need there would be for exceptions. So that we have a double jeopardy with the 1988 National Curriculum: first, its inappropriateness puts pressures on teachers to make informal and formal exceptions and second, a lack of clear, well thought out central guidance on how to make exceptions or what alternatives to use leads to confusion and anxiety.

Sections 17 and 18 of the ERA 1988, which enable formal exceptions for SEN, are so open to interpretation that they could be used to exclude many of those with SEN from much of the National Curriculum. This possibility has led to the fear, whether well-founded or not, that some pupils could be so excluded. This has been associated with the practice in many LEAs of making few, if any, formal exceptions for those with significant special educational needs. Many LEA special needs advisors and inspectors have rationalized this position in terms of the Warnock integrative philosophy. However, this has raised considerable difficulties in fully implementing the National Curriculum for teachers in ordinary and special schools.

These implementation difficulties vary according to the kind and degree of

SEN and to the location of provision. In ordinary schools, various difficulties arise. For example, there are uncertainties about the limits to the extent to which a child can be taught outside their age-relevant Key Stage. Withdrawing pupils from National Curriculum subject lessons for support can also be seen as denying them their entitlement. The main issue arises from the publication of school National Curriculum subject attainment levels, in the context of greater parental choice of schools. This puts pressure on schools to maximize attainment and schools come to reconsider pupil grouping by attainment level as a way of boosting overall attainment levels. Setting up low attainment groups could lead to some of the negative effects of 'remedial' classes on morale and attainment.

National Curriculum implementation difficulties are more extensive in special schools, even if less apparent, because they are not seen by mainstream teachers. For the reason given above, I will concentrate on the special school difficulties, which include:

(a)   lack of availability of subject staff;
(b)   lack of availability of equipment and facilities;
(c)   National Curriculum content replacing previous curriculum content perceived as more relevant;
(d)   practicality problems in using the National Curriculum in its present form:
  (i)   appropriateness of all attainment targets and programmes of study in all subjects;
  (ii) appropriateness of age-relevant Key Stage programmes of study;
  (iii) appropriateness of SATs.

These difficulties have led in a special-school context to a 'special' interpretation of what it means to apply the National Curriculum compared to ordinary schools. For example, amongst those applying the National Curriculum in special schools for severe learning difficulties, talk is about programmes of study providing experience and familiarity, not mastery or achievement of attainment levels (Ashdown, Carpenter and Bovair 1991). Applying the National Curriculum becomes a matter of experiencing attainment targets. What this usually means is that some learning activity is planned which relates loosely to the same area as the attainment target. That the National Curriculum defines attainment targets in attainment outcome terms is overlooked, as in the example of the sensory science curriculum for those with profound difficulties (Longhorn 1991). In this approach, for example, the use of finger paints and body drawing is tenuously linked to the science attainment targets 3.1a, 4.1a, 2.1a, 6.2a and 4.2a. Similarly, in the NCC materials for severe learning difficulties (NCC 1992), there is a loose notion of applying the National Curriculum. Learning activities, such as finding out which toy rolls the furthest, are linked to various National Curriculum subject programmes of study in a loose way that takes little account of how the activities will lead the pupils to attaining the relevant attainment levels.

Those who have designed the NCC approach to applying the National Curriculum to severe learning difficulties have argued against tokenism in applying it (Sebba and Clarke 1991). By this they mean that existing curricula should not be fitted to the Curriculum. Rather, they recommend that the Curriculum be examined for what is relevant to pupils with severe learning difficulties. Yet, they do not consider whether it is possible to avoid tokenism in view of the specific nature and form of the 1988 National Curriculum. I take this analysis to illustrate the need for more recognition of the tensions involved in applying the 1988 Curriculum. This will make it easier to adjust to the hard realities of making exceptions to the Curriculum in its current form, while trying to find ways of developing it to suit better the needs of those with special educational needs. In practice this will mean that selected parts of the National Curriculum will be used in special schools. This approach has been heard informally and off-the-record from some influential special educators, and is probably best expressed in Ouvry's model shown in Figure 1. This shows the National Curriculum as one of three broad sources of the special school curriculum, with what she calls the developmental and the additional curriculum, including special programmes and therapy, as other sources.

Figure 10.1 *Ouvry model of curriculum (1991).*

Though the National Curriculum needs less adapting for pupils with SEN in the ordinary school, the same basic approach in this chapter also applies. Difficulties in applying the 1988 Curriculum in ordinary schools may require adaptations which strictly speaking imply formal expectations to be recorded in Statements of SEN. Ordinary schools and LEAs may or may not follow the National Curriculum strictly for some pupils with SEN in this respect. However, what is more important is to ensure that the curriculum offered is broad and balanced and meets the general aims of education outlined in the ERA. These difficulties in applying the 1988 Curriculum present us with opportunities to review and develop its basic design.

Underlying Matters

One way of dealing with the tension between a common curriculum entitlement and meeting individual needs is to reconsider how the common entitlement is defined. In the 1988 Curriculum the common entitlement is defined by central Government in terms of programmes of study which are linked to specific attainment target levels. Of course, schools and teachers can and do influence how the National Curriculum will be applied in practice. However, with nationally prescribed SATs, the results of which will have to be published, the Government has a powerful means of central control of the Curriculum implementation. As other contributors to this book argue, planning a national curriculum as a common entitlement can be done firstly in terms of general and broad principles about what is worth learning. Once this is done the particular form it takes can then be specified. This opens the possibility of realizing a common entitlement more flexibly in a form which has particular relevance to pupils with SEN in ordinary and special schools.

Related to this matter is the way in which the Curriculum is conceptualized in terms of areas and fields of learning. The 10-level structure across subjects and phases was designed to serve the primary purpose of having an assessment-based National Curriculum. There are other options which would enable different curriculum structures for different phases of schooling. For example, the curriculum could be structured in different terms in Key Stage 1, in the infant years, and in Key Stage 4, in the last years before school leaving. This would enable a greater emphasis on social–emotional than cognitive aspects of learning in the infant years and more choice for specialization in the last years of schooling. The possibility of having different emphases at different stages of schooling would increase the relevance of a national curriculum for those with SEN.

Underlying the problem of reconciling an inclusion and an individuality principle in designing a national curriculum is the question of pupils' educational rights. There is a risk in thinking that an educational rights position means that all pupils have the right to experience the same specific curriculum as all others. In terms of the National Curriculum this could be taken to mean that all children have the right to be taught all its details. But such an entitlement would be a restraint on some pupils with significant SEN (Norwich 1990). An alternative approach is to see children as having educational rights to a relevant and worthwhile curriculum. All would be enabled to participate in a shared common framework of learning. In this formulation educational rights would be to participate in the general framework of a national curriculum and not in a specific operational version of it, like the 1988 Curriculum. This approach to rights and curricular entitlement would enable a national curriculum to better encompass the needs of those with special educational needs.

Implications for Changes to the 1988 Curriculum

What follows from this argument is the need to distinguish more thoroughly than at present between a national curriculum framework of aims and goals and the actual operational school Curriculum which embodies the framework. The national framework would be defined more fully and carefully, and with more outline of the curriculum structure and balance for different school phases. More emphasis could be placed on social and personal development and cross-curricular aspects, with a recognition of how school arrangements and ethos relate to these goals (O'Hear and White 1991). The focus of the national framework would be more on teaching than assessment, unlike the 1988 Curriculum. There would no longer be the need to have a single structure for the different areas of the National Curriculum. With less specification in detail, the responsibility would then be on the schools to design the actual operational school curriculum based on the national framework. This would also engender a greater sense of ownership by teachers who ultimately do the teaching.

Such an approach to the design of a national curriculum would provide increased flexibility to include more pupils with special educational needs and a reduced need for exceptions. The curricula of special schools could legitimately be based on a particular interpretation of the national framework relevant to significant SEN. However, to ensure that a school's actual curriculum did represent the national framework as fully as possible, there could be a requirement that schools submitted their curriculum for inspection. In the case of special schools they could explain and justify how they put the national framework into operation in ways which suited the needs of their pupils. If they could not justify their representation they could be required following an inspection to develop their curriculum in certain directions.

In moving to a more teaching-orientated national curriculum the importance of assessment would not be lessened, but assessment would not drive the design of the curriculum. Nor would a national system of assessment geared mainly for summative and evaluative purposes dominate assessment for classroom teaching purposes. There would be a move to more teacher assessment which could be moderated to ensure quality. The monitoring of local, regional or national educational standards could be conducted by the less costly random sampling of pupil attainments, along the lines of the APU. This would mean that the system of assessment for normative-teaching purposes would be separated from the system for summative-evaluative purposes. This would enable teachers to undertake additional ways of assessing the progress of children with special educational needs as part of the requirements for systematic assessment of attainments.

The moves just discussed can be represented in Figure 2, which illustrates how a national curriculum can become more focused on teaching than assessing and where control of the curriculum moves from the national level to the joint national and local school levels.

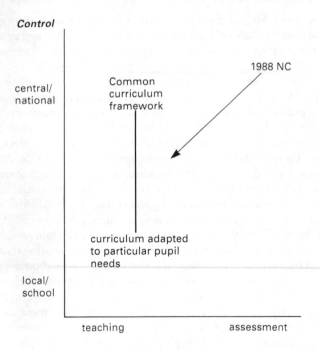

Figure 10.2   *Focus of National Curriculum design.*

Such changes would retain the advantages of the 1988 National Curriculum. The curriculum would be broad and some continuity between special and ordinary schools and units would be retained. Children with special educational needs would participate in a common curriculum entitlement and curriculum-related assessment to inform teaching and reporting to parents would be available. These changes would also avoid the overloading of the school curriculum and the excessive time taken up in national assessment. It would encourage more ownership of the National Curriculum and enable ordinary and special schools to put the National Curriculum entitlement into operation in terms which met the individual needs of those with special educational needs.

11

A Coherent Policy for Science and Technology – Some Difficulties Examined

Michael Barnett

Introduction

It is not difficult to accept that 'coherence', in some sense, is a desirable feature of a curriculum. In designing the current National Curriculum, a lot of attention has been paid to year-by-year and cross-phase progression in the delivery of individual subjects, and this could be said to impose a form of coherence on the educational process. The National Curriculum is, however, clearly weak on inter-subject coherence. The cross-curricular themes are afterthoughts – retrofitted bolt-ons, which given current realities are unlikely to be of more than ornamental significance.

There is a widespread view that coherence between science and technology is particularly desirable, perhaps even 'natural', and yet in the school curriculum, such coherence has been conspicuous mainly by its absence. Science and technology are well known to go together like fish and chips, but there are few schools in which they have ever appeared as other than chalk and cheese.

In a limited essay, it is difficult to do more than chart the obstacles in the path of this particular form of curricular convergence. It will not be a great surprise to find an unpropitious historical legacy, but beyond that, it will be necessary to look critically at the presumed 'fit' between science and technology.

Attempts to move towards inter-subject co-ordination from the starting point of a curriculum specified and delivered subject by subject must take account of distinctive, and not necessarily compatible, subject traditions. In the case of science and technology, the task is complicated by differences of status as perceived by pupils, parents and sometimes teachers themselves.

Within secondary schools, there is no very strong tradition of inter-subject co-ordination. The case is different for primary schools but it is only recently that science and technology, as a consequence of National Curriculum demands, have featured significantly in the primary school. At the same time, the statutory requirement for reporting on a subject-by-subject basis poses a threat to the primary school tradition of curriculum integration. This could be offset by the likelihood that, for economic if for no other reasons, the responsibility for co-ordinating science and for co-ordinating technology will rest with one and the same person.

The training of secondary teachers has long been organized on the basis of subject specialisms and this identification with subjects is often reinforced by the departmental structure of the school. In an era of level or declining resources, the prosperity of one subject may be predicated on the decline of others. During the expansion of technology in the last decade, schools have to some extent been cushioned from this effect by Technical and Vocational Educational Initiative (TVEI) funding. This initiative, which has also seeded significant cross-curricular innovations, has a finite life span, leaving newly created technology departments still under-resourced and in direct competition with other departments. Some degree of interdepartmental rivalry based on territoriality and self-interest is inevitable, but between science and technology, as between classics and modern languages earlier this century, there may be special aggravating factors. As Black and Harrison (1985) remind us, the pursuit of science knowledge 'is valued because it has a high status as part of a liberal curriculum', and some science teachers have been wary of becoming enmeshed or enmired with technology for fear of compromising this high status. In terms of the past tripartite system, science characterized the post-1944 grammar school, workshop skills the secondary modern school.

A Legacy of Incoherence

The historical development of science education in England and Wales demonstrates that the status of subjects can change over time. Originally a low-status subject, it has risen through the academic pecking order during this century. Government funding for science education dates from the mid-19th century and was originally intended to support night school science for artisans. The widespread acceptance, which occurred towards the turn of the century, of science in schools for the more privileged, coincided with its transformation into a liberal subject (BAAS 1889) 'taught from the first as a branch of mental education, not mainly as useful knowledge'. Even so, it was initially regarded with a mixture of suspicion and contempt.

Workshop training first appeared in elementary schools in the 1880s as what would now be called a pre-vocational initiative, i.e. with no specific occupational focus, but aiming to teach the working-class boy generic skills, e.g. 'hand-and-eye' co-ordination, precise measurement and the ability to read working drawings. Girls were treated in a more explicitly vocational manner in view of their probable destiny as paid or unpaid domestic servants, through the introduction of cookery and laundry to accompany needlework which had always been a compulsory girls' subject in elementary schools.

For more than 60 years after the 1902 Act, science teaching and craft teaching were separated not only by a chasm in esteem but also institutionally, first by the secondary/elementary divide and following 1944 by the grammar/secondary divide. The rise of the comprehensive school has reunited the two strands in institutional but not in curriculum terms or indeed in terms of status.

The last 20 years have, in fact, seen considerable developments in science education and a transformation (still in progress) of traditional craft education. It is significant, however, that despite certain attempts to stimulate convergence, the redefinition of the school subjects has led to little effective inter-penetration (McCulloch, Jenkins and Layton 1985). In science, emphasis has moved away from factual content, rote learning of definitions and taxonomies, mechanical application of formulae, etc., towards concepts, processes and scientific modes of thinking. One focus of interest, and internal tension, has been the growth of 'integrated' science at the expense of single subjects.

In its trajectory towards what is now called technology, craft was initially transformed into craft, design and technology (CDT). This involved an attempt to incorporate some elements of applied science (e.g. structures, mechanisms, electronics) but more significantly, increasing priority has been given to the active involvement of pupils in the design process with emphasis on the reflective aspects of the 'practical arts'. One hundred years ago, innovation centred on 'hand-and-eye' co-ordination, but more recently 'thought-in action' has held the stage (Kimbell *et al.* 1991). The new design-centred orthodoxy has however been subject to challenge, and the unresolved tensions between craft skills, applied science and design lie at the root of current problems in defining school technology. Other problems stem from the assumption in the National Curriculum that delivery of technology is to be shared between five previously separate subjects, namely CDT, art and design, computer studies, home economics and business studies.

Technology and Science

The elements of the O'Hear and White's (1991) curriculum earn their inclusion as a result of their presumed contribution to the formation of a citizen in a liberal democracy. Self-determination and social awareness are important goals, and both are deemed to entail an understanding of 'major industry'. It is in the context of 'industrial understanding' both at home and overseas (O'Hear and White 1991, pp. 14–15), that technology, science and maths are seen as necessary curriculum elements. O'Hear and White offer no further pointers to conceptualizing the curricular relationship between science and technology.

It could be presumed, however, that since 'major industry' is an important site of technological activity, that a 'technology-led' version of the science/

technology relationship is implied, i.e. that science should appear in the curriculum mainly as a function of its applicability to technology. It can be argued that this does not necessarily place a gross restriction on the scope of school science and that in the context of modern technology, scientific concepts such as fields, waves, atoms, molecules, energy levels, etc. are just as relevant to an understanding of the made world as they are to the analysis of natural phenomena. Consideration of the concept of a technology-led programme is a convenient way of raising some of the curriculum design issues associated with the co-ordination of science and technology.

It should be emphasized at the outset that, as might easily be inferred from the historical account given earlier, the notion of science appearing mainly or solely as ancillary to technology has no major historical precedent within the British school system, either in the pre- or post-compulsory phase. In full-time post-compulsory schooling, the most usual assumption has been that science and technology will ultimately be brought into relationship within higher education, for those students going on to specialize in e.g. engineering and medicine. In this context, sixth-form maths, physics, chemistry and biology constitute pre-vocational preparation.

We should note, however, that minor and largely forgotten tradition of the secondary technical school – the thin layer of meat in the post-1944 tripartite sandwich. In this ill-fated sector, it could be argued that science programmes were more or less explicitly designed with applicability to industrial practice in mind. An applied science textbook (Brown and Jones 1939) used in technical schools 50 years ago gives as its aim, 'to illustrate principles by their application to working practice, in order to create interest as well as stimulate thought', and adopts a treatment 'such as to enable students to understand those practical applications likely to come within their working experience'.

It can be seen that this embodied, in common with many 'academic' science courses, an approach which travelled from principles towards applications. The vocational focus, however, lent the destinations greater significance, and in consequence, applications tended to be treated more seriously than they could have been within the liberally conceived science courses of the mainstream tradition.

The notion of a technology-led science provision suggests the possibility of inverting the conventional relationship between 'pure' and 'applied' science, i.e. to not, figuratively speaking, work outwards from principles to applications, but to take context and application as the starting points and to work inside towards the necessary concepts and principles. This 'outside-in' approach to science could reasonably be predicted to be more motivating. It is not necessarily a sign of 'academic weakness' to wish to know the point of what one is studying.

We now need to examine the problems posed to the curriculum designer seeking to co-ordinate science and technology in the context of technologies significant to modern industry. This requires some discussion of the role of science in modern technology.

It is quite common to identify technology with applied science but this is, at best, a half-truth. Black and Harrison (1985) make a useful distinction between 'contrivance' technology, 'exemplified by many gifted engineers in the last century, who worked with no formal scientific understanding of their problems', and 'applied science' technology 'in which one increasingly needs to grasp the conceptual science even to understand the problem'.

The distinction between science-rich and virtually science-free technology is perhaps not as sharp as this simple dichotomy might imply, but the middle range of the continuum from 'contrivance' to 'applied science' technology is somewhat sparsely occupied. An appreciable fraction of economically significant technology makes relatively few demands on scientific understanding. In schools, the activities currently labelled 'technology', for many of which convincing arguments for curriculum inclusion can be made, come from the 'contrivance' end of this continuum. At the other extreme lie the 'key technologies' (FEU 1988) associated with contemporary industrial innovation, for which modern science of an advanced and sophisticated nature forms a key resource.

The problem for curriculum design is that while in no circumstances can technology be reduced to the 'appliance of science', much modern technology makes extensive use of scientific knowledge, and moreover makes quite promiscuous use of it, with no regard for the convenience of those concerned with designing coherence and progression into a programme of study for science. Typically, the 'key science' underpinning 'key technologies' embraces a number of distinct principles presenting problems at different levels of conceptual difficulty. Insight into some aspects of a device or system might result from relatively simple scientific understandings. Other aspects would typically be some way beyond the scope of school science.

For example, a good deal about an incandescent lamp, rather less about a discharge lamp and very little about a laser can be understood on a basis of elementary science. How and why these three important light sources differ from one another taxes the understanding of most physics undergraduates. Likewise, numerous scientific principles and effects are embodied in the design and operation of a coloured cathode-ray tube display, as employed in most television receivers and many desk-top computer systems. Some of these can be fairly readily explained at an elementary level and others cannot. The general point to be made is that the technological coherence gained by focusing on a particular set of artefacts, techniques or applications may be gained at the expense of fragmentation and incoherence in the presentation of science. In addition, too specific a technological focus may serve to obscure the fact that the great *practical* utility of science derives from its power to abstract and generalize, whereby insights and modes of analysis developed in one context can often be adapted for creative use in others.

In practice, coherence between science and technology is most clearly demonstrated in advanced contexts such as the research and development sections of high-tech industries or the instrumentation facilities and projects associated with 'big' science. In these contexts, there is exhibited what David Layton (1988) has characterized as a 'complex, symbiotic and egalitarian' relationship between science and technology. In educational settings marked 'technology-led', coherence is only to be found in engineering higher education (HE). Here it is normally assumed that entrants will previously have studied maths and pure science, without any particular technological focus. Up to now there has been no very strong pressure from HE for a co-ordinated approach to science and technology at a school level. Thus progression to HE is premised on the acceptance of a traditional view of science teaching criticized by Black and Harrison (1985):

> *Typical of this traditional posture has been the view that school science is all preparatory and the belief that pupils cannot attempt open-ended or project work, or study current pure research or engineering, because more work is needed on basic principles.*

Any serious attempt to co-ordinate science and technology at a school level implies a rejection of that view. However, as the preceding discussion should have made clear, it is easier to agree on the desirability of a co-ordinated programme around 'real-world' applications than to actually design and deliver such a programme. The fact that the 'fit' between science and technology is most natural in advanced contexts means that in general, co-ordination should be less difficult in the later stages of schooling (14–18 years old). At an earlier stage, co-ordination will have to be bought at the expense of artificiality and contrivance, and it may be a matter of judgement as to whether this price is worth paying.

Which Way Now?

For those who regard curricular convergence between science and technology as educationally progressive, the current National Curriculum represents several steps backwards. Several references have already been made to Black and Harrison's 1985 paper *In Place of Confusion* which advocated a radically revised curriculum model which might facilitate convergence. Within their scheme, tasks, assignments and projects were to have equal status with 'resources' which were to be quarried from the traditional subject areas. Even then, the authors were in no doubt about the likely difficulties.

> *Many still feel that these proposals have an air of unreality about them. . . . To ask for a change of attitude on such fundamental issues is to ask for a very great deal.*

In 1992 a subject-based curriculum is statutory and there seems little official enthusiasm for project-based delivery. Reformers, to quote the well-worn phrase, would 'rather not be starting from here'. In the area of science and technology, the confusion perceived by Black and Harrison has been considerably compounded. It has been suggested (Smithers and Robinson 1992), on scant evidence, that they are partly to blame for this. What is undeniable is that the science Order has already undergone a much criticized revision and that the technology Order is being revised by HMI. Co-ordination with the maths and science Orders forms part of the terms of reference for the review.

A number of authors (Smithers and Robinson 1992, Barlex 1990, Barnett 1992) have drawn attention to the weakness of the applied science strands in National Curriculum technology, notwithstanding the wording of the original brief of the Working Party in which it is stated that technology is that area of the curriculum where pupils 'draw on knowledge and skills from a range of subjects but always from science and mathematics'.

Now, as we have seen, the issues here are far from simple. Much designing and making necessarily involves elementary maths but no appreciable input from science. A curriculum which insists on nothing but 'applied science' technology will look quite different from one which relaxes that restriction, and will, in any case, be a non-starter before Key Stage 4. A case could be made however for making some measure of 'applied-science' technology or 'technologically-referenced' science a mandatory element of the 14-plus curriculum. Before this could be a reality, a number of issues would need to be addressed, which are now listed together with brief comments on each.

Curriculum Design

The National Curriculum was designed with little or no reference to issues of progression at 16-plus. There are now indications that official thinking is starting to focus on 14–18 as a basis for planning. Any new initiative in the area of science/technology would have to take account of developments in Key Stage 4 and General National Vocational Qualifications (gNVQ), where many significant details have yet to emerge.

Another important issue arises from the need to cater for both intending specialists and non-specialist, and the extent to which there could/should be common programmes. Is it, for instance, possible to specify a 'core' entitlement in post-16 science and technology? How might/should this relate to programmes in science, technology and society, and economic and industrial understanding?

A further significant issue concerns co-ordination with teaching and learning in mathematics. It is already acknowledged that, particularly in the context of progression to HE in engineering, foundation mathematics is an urgent developmental priority.

Curriculum Support Materials

Major activity is required in this area, and there are few precedents. It might be useful to revisit the texts of the technical school era. More generally an evaluation of the strengths and shortcomings of the science components of existing vocational qualifications would be useful.

One curriculum project which has adopted an 'outside-in' approach to science is Salters' Science, developed by the Science Education Group at the University of York. There is a GCSE programme and a well-regarded A-level chemistry programme. The same group is presently engaged in the development of a post-16 Science in the Environment programme which may provide pointers to devising a science 'core' for non-specialists and strategies for designing science-in-technology packages.

Another relevant project, still in its development phase, is Nuffield financed and is intended to support the delivery of National Curriculum technology. In this programme an attempt is being made to hold in balance the craft, design and applied science aspects of school technology. Mention should also be made of the recently started 14–19 Science with Technology project, jointly sponsored by ASE and DATA.

Professional Development

National Curriculum technology, despite clear warnings of the serious consequences of so doing, was launched without adequate INSET support. Subsequent events have shown the warnings to have been amply justified.

Who is to teach any newly developed programmes linking science and technology in the context of industrial understanding? Few science teachers have any industrial experience; few teachers of technology have any very substantial acquaintance with science.

Education–Industry Links

A curriculum which sets up understanding major industries as a major aim will require major industrial participation in its design and delivery. Every secondary school needs organic, self-sustaining and long-term industrial links.

Progress towards curricular coherence between science and technology requires, therefore, a number of properly resourced and researched interventions and initiatives, implying sustained investment over a long period. In the current political and economic climate, this is asking for a great deal, but nothing less will do. In this context, O'Hear and White's 5-year 'timetable for change' looks markedly optimistic.

12

The Arts in the National Curriculum: Which Way Now?

Ken Robinson

The spirits of many arts teachers are at a low ebb. They have good reason. Although there is some provision for the arts in the National Curriculum, the burden of the Government's reforms in education seems to weigh against many of the interests and values of arts education. The arts were the last subjects to be specified in the Orders: the Orders themselves for the arts are less specific than for all other National Curriculum subjects. Art and music have become the only optional foundation subjects for 14–16-year-olds. This was the previous Secretary of State's uninspired and unsurprising solution to the congestion that the Government itself had imposed on Key Stage 4. The dissolution of LEA central services has minimized the systems of support on which the development of the arts in schools had relied – local advisers, arts resource centres and peripatetic specialists. On top of this, the management of delegated budgets is threatening the position of some specialist arts teachers, especially in dance and drama.

All of this seems conclusively depressing, and some of it certainly is. During the past 20 years, arts teaching has been making impressive strides in schools. A full arts curriculum has been increasingly recognized as a central element in the intellectual and aesthetic development of all young people, and in the educational vitality of the school as a whole. The present depression of arts teaching may not have been the direct intention of the Government's programme, but it is undoubtedly one of its effects. Arts teachers now face a complicated and daunting task. They need to sustain, and in some cases resurrect, a coherent programme of arts education in the context of a National Curriculum whose provision for the arts is radically incoherent. What should they do? In moving forward, arts teachers, and arts educators more generally, need to address four pressing questions: Why are the arts poorly provided for in the National Curriculum? What room is there for improvement? What improvements are needed? How can improvements be brought about?

What's the Problem?

Arts education suffers from a curious political ambivalence. While the products of artistic practice are highly regarded, the processes that achieve them are not. Arts teachers often complain of the low status of the arts in education. The inadequate provisions of the National Curriculum seem to support this view. Is it wholly true? Outside schools, the arts have high social and political status. The artist in Western culture is an exalted figure. A knowledge and appreciation of the arts is firmly associated with an educated mind and a cultivated sensibility. The arts excite strong political views. A Secretary of State can guarantee headlines and, with luck, a furore simply by proposing which works of literature, art or music should be taught in schools, and which not. None of this suggests that the arts are politically unimportant. Yet the arts have had a poor deal in the National Curriculum, and their position seems to be deteriorating. Why is this?

Part of the reason is that there are two distinct, though related, agendas in the present political programme for education. The status of the arts in schools is ambiguous because they are seen as central to one and marginal to the other. The first is concerned with intellectual development and attainment. This 'attainment' agenda is clearly illustrated in the political concern with literacy, numeracy, national testing and A-levels. No serious commentator doubts the importance of developing children's intellectual capabilities to their limits, nor the importance of thorough and reliable assessment procedures. The problem for the arts lies in the dominant conceptions of intelligence and modes of assessment that have shaped the National Curriculum. In the national debate on education, and certainly in the present legislation, the arts have rarely been linked with the attainment agenda.

In his speech to the North of England conference in January 1992, Kenneth Clarke began by emphasizing the importance to the nation of developing its 'brains'. He went on to announce, 10 minutes later, that art and music were no longer to be compulsory in the National Curriculum. There was no reaction to this. This is because intelligence, 'brains', in the political mind is still almost exclusively associated with verbal and mathematical reasoning and with propositional knowledge. Practical work in the arts is not so much associated with intelligence, which schools are required to develop, as with talent, which they might choose to encourage.

The second agenda is concerned with cultural identity and conceptions of heritage. The arts are seen as central to the cultural agenda of education. Canonical works of literature, music and the visual arts are highly valued both in themselves and also as bearing many of the cultural genes by which the nation's identity is passed from one generation to the next. For this reason, the content, if not the process of arts education, is hotly contested. The political interest in the cultural content of arts education presents different difficulties for different teachers. For some, the emphasis on Western culture in culturally diverse schools presents ethical as well as canonical issues. For others, the principal value of arts education lies in the processes of personal creativity and expression. The issue for them is not which cultural products to teach but whether cultural transmission is the purpose of arts education at all.

What are the Opportunities?

For the past 2 years or so there has been a necessary preoccupation among arts educators with influencing the Orders for the arts in the National Curriculum and with issues of national policy. The debate must now focus on influencing provision in individual schools. The National Curriculum is not yet a straitjacket. Despite common assumptions to the contrary, all schools continue to have considerable discretion over the structure, organization and content of the curriculum. In the present legislation, the Secretary of State may not prescribe how much time is spent on any aspect of the curriculum, nor how the curriculum is organized.

In the Orders, dance is treated as part of PE. But if a school decides to have dance as a separate subject on the curriculum, it can: if it wants to have drama as a separate subject, it can.

Moreover, the Orders are more relaxed than for other subjects. On the one hand, this provides a weaker statutory framework to protect the arts: on the other, it gives schools and teachers more freedom to develop their work as they choose. How the National Curriculum is taught is still for individual schools to determine; and, although it seems taunting to be reminded of it, the National Curriculum is still not the whole curriculum. A school could base its entire curriculum on the arts if it chose to, or even become a specialist centre for the arts.

How a school provides for the arts is not only a matter of curriculum design. The National Curriculum is only one of the new dynamics in education. The interaction between the National Curriculum and LMS will be a key factor in determining the future shape of the curriculum in each school. School governors are empowered to organize the curriculum and deploy the school's resources as they see fit to meet their statutory obligations. This is a genuine opportunity for the arts in schools: it is also a potential danger. Schools are having mixed fortunes under LMS. For all schools the largest proportion of the devolved budget is spent on staff costs. Sometimes the only way to make ends meet is to lose or downgrade a teaching post. There is evidence already that some schools are preferring to employ less experienced, less expensive staff. In deciding which posts to cut, governors may well look first to their most demanding statutory responsibilities. For this reason we may begin to see a gradual erosion of specialist drama and dance posts. A minimalist reading of the National Curriculum, combined with the exigencies of LMS, will produce an impoverished arts education. It is for the teachers concerned to advocate the benefits to the school as a whole of a more expansive arts policy. What should it include?

What Improvements are Needed?

In order to improve provision for the arts, teachers and schools must know what kind of arts provision they want. Conceptions of the shape and content of the arts curriculum are sharply contested. There are divisions among arts educators over whether some arts disciplines are more important to pupils' development than others; whether art and design, for example, is of more value to more pupils than say dance or drama. There is contention over whether arts specialists should collaborate in their teaching, and if so, when, why and in what ways. There is particular disagreement about the nature and importance of combined arts courses and their relationship to specialist teaching. Is it reasonable to talk of a policy for the arts in general in schools, as it seems to be to talk of a general policy for science education? Or are the different arts disciplines discrete and to be taught separately? These issues need to be faced in schools in the interests of an arts education which is well founded conceptually, and coherent in practice.

I said earlier that the framing of the National Curriculum is radically incoherent. This is true in terms of both the attainment and the cultural agendas. The National Curriculum proposes that there are five art forms. Two of these, art and music, are seen as free-standing foundation subjects and of fundamental importance to all young people, at least to the age of 14. Two of them, drama and dance, are seen as branches of other subjects, English and PE. These are also important for all pupils, but only until they are 14. The fifth, literature, is part of English too, but this matters until they are 16. English encompasses media education, including films and television, and these also matter to the age of 16. This framing of the arts is inadequate for two reasons. First, it is a rigid and narrow conception of the arts themselves. For this reason, it is inadequate for the cultural agenda of education. Second, it does not recognize the differing aptitudes and abilities of pupils and is therefore inadequate for the attainment agenda.

The framing of the arts in the National Curriculum is not unusual. Most European countries that provide for the arts in schools follow a similar pattern, as do the USA and Canada. Nor is it accidental. In the United Kingdom, art and music have long been established in most schools. Among the arts, they have the best organized and largest subject associations. Historically, drama does have a long-standing association with English teaching, as does dance with PE. But habits can change. During the past 20 years, many secondary schools have set up separate drama departments and employed specialist drama teachers. More recently, dance has begun to claim and win similar recognition. Schools were also developing initiatives that brought the arts together in various ways, from joint projects to single faculties. This is not the place to rehearse again the educational arguments for or against the arts in general or for individual disciplines. It is a place to note that the proposals for the arts in the National Curriculum did not rehearse any arguments at all, one way or the other, for enforcing the habitual divisions between art and music, dance and drama. This classification was simply taken for granted. This division of the arts into three major art forms and two minor ones compares poorly to the diversity and dynamism of the arts as they occur outside schools.

There are and have been a multiplicity of art forms, in Western European and other cultures. It would be hard to say how many, but it is more than five. The forms of arts practice are influenced by contemporary values and conventions. They are also influenced by the availability of tools, materials and techniques: that is, by technology. The classical tradition in European music was facilitated by the technologies of instrument manufacture, just as contemporary innovations in electronic music have been facilitated by the microchip. Art is not exclusive to particular tools or materials: it is made from whatever materials artists use. A contemporary list of art forms should recognize the impact of contemporary technologies on the present varieties of arts practice, including the applications of video, film, television, computers, digital synthesizers, and so on. It should recognize that artists may work in several media for the same project, or combine techniques from several previously distinct forms to generate new forms of practice: as in performance art, installations, sign dancing, performance poetry. Some traditional art forms were always multi-media. Theatre uses language, movement, visual imagery and the rhythms of space and time to achieve its effects, just as these are used separately in literature, dance, painting, sculpture and music to achieve theirs. Dance in performance is as much a visual art for the audience as it is a physical experience for the dancers. It is created in one mode and received in another. These complex dynamics of the arts in practice must be allowed for in the organization of the arts in education.

There are commanding problems in the organization of any curriculum. It has to function as an adequate model of knowledge and experience, in a world where the boundaries of knowledge are provisional and constantly extending. It has to enable the practical tasks of teaching to be divided between the teachers available, and to make acceptable use of their expertise. As a result, the planning of a curriculum falls somewhere between epistemology and logistics. In addition, and in secondary schools especially, teachers derive their professional identity from what they teach rather than who they teach. This makes the pull of the subject very strong indeed.

In NCC (1990d) we reflected on the difficulties of describing the arts curriculum in terms of lists of art forms. We proposed that the curriculum should provide opportunities for all pupils to work in a range of different *modes* of practice: the *visual, aural, verbal, kinaesthetic* and *enactive*. This formulation differs from the National Curriculum's approach in that it gives equal importance to each of these modes. A principal reason is that individuals have different capacities in different modes of practice and understanding. Strength in one does not entail strength in another. Some individuals come alive in the visual mode, possibly in a range of art forms, others in the kinaesthetic mode, in dance, mime or movement. But musicians may not be dancers, or painters. The reason for pressing for a common policy for the arts in general in schools is not to blur the distinctions between legitimate specialisms. It is to ensure that the provision is co-ordinated to meet the needs and abilities of individuals. It is an argument for differentiation not for homogeneity. It is this principle that has been sacrificed by the Secretary of State in making some of the arts optional at age 14. The opportunity to pursue specialist interests in the arts beyond 14 as part of the compulsory curriculum must be pressed in any future review of Key Stage 4.

Which Way Now?

I began by saying that the national political programme for education includes two distinct agendas. Arts educators have three: conceptual, political and practical. The conceptual agenda is concerned with clarifying and, so far as possible, agreeing on issues of purpose, structure and content in the arts curriculum. The political agenda is concerned with affecting the perceptions and actions of those who can facilitate change. These now include, critically, the governors and parents of individual schools with their new powers of self-determination. The practical agenda involves mobilizing resources. The most important resource in education is teachers. Arts education has a problem in this respect, especially in Key Stages 1 and 2.

The common response of primary school teachers to the Orders for the arts in the National Curriculum is anxiety bred from lack of confidence. The Orders propose that children learn skills in and knowledge about the arts which general classroom teachers often do not have themselves. Encouraging teachers beyond the National Curriculum will be difficult when they feel daunted by its present demands. There are primary teachers with specialist training in the arts and they feel more comfortable. But teachers with specialist training in other areas of the curriculum often worry that they need to be artists themselves before they can teach the arts. To an extent this is true. They do need to know about the processes of the arts, and about the aims and principles of arts education. Good arts teachers have an enthusiasm for their disciplines which all good teachers have. But it underestimates the arts to suppose that they can be taught from a base of enthusiasm alone. The development of the arts in the primary school will have to be supported by sharply focused in-service training in the arts.

Changes in HE and in the training of teachers may make possible new patterns of in-service provision and continuing professional development which help to bridge the traditional divide between training, research and curriculum development. At present, students spend 4 years in initial training and subsequently have occasional periods of in-service training. We should move to a situation where teachers maintain relationships with HE institutions through further courses which add progressively to their professional qualifications. They may continue to work towards professional diplomas or higher degrees which may include substantial components of school-based research and development. In these ways, HE in partnership with schools may be able to fill part of the vacuum in school-based support that has been caused by the collapse of the LEA advisory services on which the historical development of the arts in schools relied.

The spirits of many arts teachers are at a low ebb, just as the spirits of many other teachers have been sapped by the practical demands and political rhetoric of the last 4 years. But tides eventually turn. There have been gains for the arts in the National Curriculum as well as losses and these must be built on. The task for all arts teachers now is to convince their own schools that the National Curriculum is a starting point for the development of the arts in schools and not a conclusion. They should begin by convincing each other.

13

Provision for Personal and Social Development through the Cross-Curricular Themes: A Framework

Martin Buck and Sally Inman

This paper outlines the provision for personal and social development of pupils within the current legislative context and offers a planning framework by which the cross-curricular themes can provide for effective personal and social development within the taught curriculum. The paper is an edited extract from Buck and Inman (1992).

Personal and Social Development within ERA

The aims of the 1988 ERA cannot be met without explicit provision for the personal and social development of pupils. The aims specify that pupils' education must be broad and balanced, i.e. core and foundation are the minimum entitlement; it must attend to the development of the whole child; and it must have relevance both for pupils' current lives and for their lives in the future. Any entitlement curriculum must therefore take serious account of these aims. What has subsequently become clear is the need for schools to ensure that provision for personal and social development is made central to whole-school planning, rather than being assumed or somehow tacked on. The NCC in Circular 6 and Curriculum Guidance 3 (NCC 1990a, b) have articulated the importance of whole-school planning in relation to personal and social development. Thus we have a statutory requirement to ensure an entitlement curriculum in which there is clear timetabled and non-timetabled provision for the personal and social development of pupils. More specifically, this should be achieved through whole-school curriculum planning, i.e. provision should be explicitly planned for within core and foundation subjects, religious education, additional subjects, as well as through extra-curricular activities, school ethos and other important aspects of school life.

Personal and Social Development and the Cross-Curricular Elements

If the NCC envisage schools making provision for personal and social development as part of whole-school curriculum planning, then the three identified cross-curricular elements are seen as central to this provision. Thus personal and social development is located within the way in which the dimensions, skills and themes underpin, and are embedded within, all aspects of whole-school policies – the taught curriculum, extra-curricular activities, pastoral, assemblies, etc., as well as being an explicit part of the ethos of every school. Within the taught curriculum, the delivery of the five cross-curricular themes can be seen as critical for this will provide much of the provision for personal and social development within this area.

NCC (1990b) outlined the role and nature of the cross-curricular dimensions, skills and themes. Dimensions such as multiculturalism and equal opportunities are described as extending beyond the taught curriculum, as major aspects of the whole life of a school. They should embrace lessons, assemblies, tutorial programmes, mandatory out of school activities such as residential courses, clubs, games, and the 'hidden curriculum' of school ethos, rules, expectations and relationships. Skills, such as communication, IT, numeracy, personal and social, should be explicitly built into all areas of the taught curriculum but also, like the dimensions, should extend into all areas of school activities. The themes such as health education and environmental education are seen as providing central cross-curricular areas of knowledge, skills, understanding, value and attitude formation. Whilst the themes are not restricted to the taught curriculum they will form a major part of taught curriculum provision for personal and social development.

The Issues for Schools

Schools then face a number of issues and challenges:

How do they conceive of the personal and social development of pupils within their school? What qualities and skills do they wish young people to acquire and what processes would best effect their acquisition?

How will they ensure that this conception of personal and social development is explicitly embedded within whole curriculum planning?

How will they ensure that the cross-curricular elements are effectively used as the statutory device by which pupils are guaranteed this vital part of their educational entitlement?

Within the taught curriculum how will they ensure delivery of the themes in ways which enable this personal and social development to take place?

In trying to meet these challenges schools may understandably turn to bodies such as the NCC for help and guidance in areas such as defining personal and social development, whole-curriculum planning, providing coherence through cross-curricular elements. We want to look briefly at the guidance available to teachers on some of these critical areas.

What is personal and social development?

How should schools begin to clarify what might be meant by the personal and social development of pupils? If we turn to the NCC documentation for guidance we find the following statement.

The education system is charged with preparing young people to take their place in a wide range of roles in adult life. It also has a duty to educate the individuals to be able to think and act for themselves, with an acceptable set of personal qualities and values which also meet the wider social demands of adult life. In short the personal and social development of pupils is a major aim of education; personal and social education the means by which this aim is achieved.

(NCC 1990b)

At first glance this may seem to provide a useful framework, but when we look at it more closely it perhaps raises more questions than it provides answers. As teachers we have to be clear as to what we mean by 'acceptable personal qualities and values' in young people – acceptable to whom? What is meant by the 'wider social demands of adult life'? Are the demands likely to be the same for all young people, or are they not at least partly dependent on factors such as gender, economic circumstance, race? What does it mean for young people to 'think and act for themselves'? The statement from the NCC glosses over important issues about the balance between self-interest and the constraints necessary for co-operative living. There is no reference either to the fact that there are wider societal factors which may critically affect a young person's ability to 'think and act for themselves', e.g. family structure, cultural contexts, gender divisions. As these terms stand with NCC (1990b) they are open to a multitude of potentially conflicting meanings and practices (see Buck and Inman 1992 for a detailed model).

Providing coherence and wholeness – a 'bolt on' approach

Whilst the NCC requires schools to take whole-school curriculum planning seriously there has been little useful guidance as to how schools can begin this process. The reason for this lack of effective guidance from this and other bodies can, at least in part, be explained by the 'bolt on' nature of these whole-school and cross-curricular planning initiatives. It is difficult to expect schools to take such a challenge seriously when it clearly comes as an afterthought, as a way of producing coherence and wholeness in a curriculum which is increasingly fragmented and narrowly subject led. In 1990 the NCC described the cross-circular elements as the parts which will 'bond' the new curriculum together, i.e. will produce the wholeness. This statement might have been more believable if those elements had, from the outset, been explicitly promoted as a central cohesive force within the National Curriculum. As it was, teachers could be forgiven for thinking that the cross-curricular elements were something to be tacked on to the real curriculum which was seen in terms of the core and foundation subjects.

The NCC guidance for the five themes

The problems facing teachers who wish to promote curriculum wholeness and coherence through the use of the cross-curricular elements have not been made easier by the nature of the NCC guidance for the themes. The areas of knowledge, understanding, skills, etc. covered by the five themes are obviously not mutually exclusive; there are significant overlaps between them and yet the guidance documents provide little useful advice as to how teachers might make these links explicit in the planning and delivery of the themes. In fact, the guidance documents intensify the difficulties since there is no coherence of approach or perspective across the five documents.

Challenge and Coherence for Pupils through the Themes

The lack of coherence in the NCC guidance necessitates that, in the planning and teaching strategies we adopt to deliver the themes, we ourselves find mechanisms to effect coherence between them. Coherence must be built at the point of planning and must enable the learner to understand the interrelationships between the different aspects of the world that are encompassed by the themes.

The subject matter of the cross-curricular themes is manifestly relevant and meaningful, but modes of delivery must also present pupils with such intellectual challenge as is appropriate for their stage of development. We must ensure that any provision includes a body of knowledge: young people's understanding of themselves cannot take place in a vacuum but must be set within the context of knowledge of their family, community, nation and the wider world in which they live. It is through an understanding of the social, economic, political and environmental aspects of the world that they come to develop and understand their own personal qualities, attitudes and values. It is through this form of understanding that young people are empowered to act in an informed and purposeful manner. This form of understanding also requires a particular teaching and learning style – one which is participatory and experiential. However, as HMI inspections of PSE courses have indicated, the quality of the learning is impaired where emphasis on the process is not matched by equal stress on content and where there is not a clearly articulated relationship between the two (Shelton 1990).

What we are advocating then is a form of learning which enables pupils to acquire knowledge through a focus upon content which is challenging and relevant and learning processes which are active and experiential.

Taught provision for personal and social development through the themes should provide challenge and coherence. It is our view that in order to provide this the forms of delivery must meet four important criteria: an objective approach to issues and evidence; the use of concepts; participatory and experiential teaching and learning styles; and the exploration of key questions and issues. We develop these criteria as follows:

Criterion 1 – Objectivity and the use of evidence. The cross-curricular themes relate to important aspects of pupils' experience, and of the world in which they live. The themes cannot avoid dealing with values and questions of morality and will, at times, involve tackling controversial issues. Therefore, it is important for us to encourage an open-minded approach to issues and a respect for evidence in formulating judgements and responding to those of others. This involves:

(a) Helping young people to understand that there is a range of ways of life within their own society and throughout the world.

(b) Encouraging a critical perspective, one in which explanations are sought for trends, patterns and events and which enables pupils to question and investigate social arrangements which have been traditionally taken for granted.

(c) Enabling pupils to judge the quality and quantity of evidence, rather than accepting it at face value. It is our view that this approach to evidence enables pupils to challenge their own assumptions and those of others and to put their own experience within the wider societal and international context.

Criterion 2 – Using concepts. We see concepts as the intellectual building blocks by which pupils can be enabled to analyse the important questions and issues that confront them now and in the future. Concepts are essential aids to the categorization, organization and analysis of knowledge and experiences.

Criterion 3 – Participatory and experiential teaching and learning styles. In our delivery of the themes we must ensure that we explicitly and systematically build in opportunities for pupils to become participants in and responsible for their own learning – to help them to become independent learners. The learning processes must develop a range of skills: IT, communication, decision-making, personal and social, study, etc.

Criterion 4 – Key questions and issues. We must ensure that we encourage pupils to deal explicitly with questions and issues that enable them to explore fundamental aspects of our lives. The cross-curricular themes have the capacity to explore critical aspects of the way we see ourselves and behave towards each other, the ways we organize collective living, and the quality of life in our own and other societies. The focus on questions and issues also provides coherence across the themes and a challenge to teaching and learning.

A Framework for Delivering the Cross-Curricular Elements within the Taught Curriculum

The framework seeks to provide guidance as to how we might deliver the cross-curricular themes within the taught curriculum in ways which meet the criteria. The framework is organized around nine central questions. Each question is then explored through a set of organizing ideas and is accompanied by a list of the concepts which we have identified as useful tools for examining the question. For each question and set of organizing ideas we have attempted to direct teachers to examples of more substantive areas of content which can serve as vehicles for more in-depth examination of the ideas. We have linked these areas to the five cross-curriculum themes and tried to show how, through exploring such content, we can deliver much of the NCC guidance documents for each theme within an integrated framework.

For each area we have indicated which particular aspects of the guidance documents we are covering and noted the Key Stages where appropriate. However, we should stress that the noting of the Key Stages does not necessarily imply that we should uncritically accept the documents' views as to what pupils should know or can handle at different ages. Whilst we have deliberately linked the ideas and content to the document so as to provide for a more critical approach to the guidance, this should not prevent us from examining areas of the themes excluded from the documents. Nor should it preclude us from including examination of other equally important cross-circular themes such as media education or development education. We hope that the framework has the flexibility to do this.

The framework is not in the nature of a syllabus or course but, rather, is intended primarily as a planning and teaching tool. We hope that it will assist teachers to identify some of the central questions and issues embedded in all the themes and to find ways of building these in their curriculum provision. The framework has been written for use at both primary and secondary level since the questions and ideas within it are as pertinent for 5-year-old pupils as they are for 16-year-olds. However, they would clearly be tackled in different ways and at different levels of complexity with different ages so as to ensure progression. We would envisage that some of the organizing ideas can be addressed more directly with older students.

The nine central questions are:

(1) What is the nature of our rights and responsibilities in everyday life? This question explores individuals' rights and responsibilities as members of families, as employers and employees, as consumers and as citizens of a particular country and of the world.

(2) On what basis do people influence and control others? This question explores the different ways people have power and authority. For example, through work, religious practice, politics. It looks at people's ability to make decisions and how these decisions affect their own lives and the lives of others.

(3) What is the balance between individual freedom and the constraints necessary for co-operative living? This question explores some of the consequences which arise from the choices people make for themselves and for others. For example, the consequences of different economic and political policies for people's work, leisure, health, etc.

(4) In what ways do people organize, manage and control their relationships? This question explores relationships between people and between countries. It looks at how and why conflict or co-operation between people can operate within domestic situations, within community affairs and in international relations.

(5) In what ways are people different and with what consequences? This question explores how differences and inequalities between people, groups and nations can be reinforced or reduced by our attitudes, ideas and actions.

(6) How do people learn the requirements of a particular culture? This question explores how we learn attitudes, beliefs and values through families, the media, education and the wider culture(s) in which we live.

(7) What constitutes a community; how are communities organized? This question explores how communities are made up of people and the built and the natural environment. It looks at the decisions that are made within communities, for example, about employment, homes, leisure and health provision.

(8) In what ways are the welfare of individuals and societies maintained? This question explores how physical and mental health, the quality of the environment, income and wealth together make up people's welfare. It looks at the responsibilities people have for their own welfare and for the welfare of others.

(9) On what basis do people make decisions when faced with particular choices? This question explores how people make choices about their family lives, their work, in buying goods and services, in their leisure activities. It looks at the effects of the choices made – for the individual, for others, and on the environment.

Developing a Question in Terms of Ideas, Concepts and Themes

We now give an example of the questions together with the organizing ideas, concepts and the links to the cross-curricular themes.

What is the balance between individual freedom and the constraints necessary for co-operative living?

(a) *Organizing ideas:* Individuals make choices about different aspects of their lives, but in the context of the needs and rights of others. There is sometimes a tension between the individual's freedom to make such choices and the needs and rights of others. Government and the law can play an important role in effecting a balance between individual freedom and the rights of others. Government have different views as to how best to preserve the freedom of the individual and satisfy the needs of society.

(b) *Concepts:* The central concepts for this question are Freedom and Constraint but other concepts may be useful in exploring this question. These include: rights, responsibility, welfare, health.

(c) *Links to the cross-curricular themes:* Personal freedoms to make choices about areas such as personal life styles, family structures, careers (*careers education, Key Stages 2–4; health education; family life and aspects of sex education; citizenship: family*). The tensions between individual freedoms and the needs and rights of others and the attempts to balance these through social convention and through legislation in areas such as race relations, equal opportunities, industrial relations, child protection, the environment (*citizenship: family and work, employment and leisure; environmental education; economic and industrial understanding, Key Stages 2–4*). The role of governments, EC, UNO and other international bodies in work, employment and economic policy (*citizenship: work, employment and leisure; economic and industrial understanding, Key Stages 2–4*). The effect of different Government policies, managerial decisions and industrial action upon individual groups, societies and on the environment as seen in areas such as health, employment, wealth distribution, conservation (*economic and industrial understanding, Key Stages 2–4; environmental education; health education: environmental aspects*).

Managing the Cross-curricular Framework

The framework we have outlined enables school managers to ask fundamental questions about a school's commitment to the personal and social development of pupils and to reflect critically upon the appropriate organizational and management structure to support this. Schools will need to review their aims and policies for personal and social development in the light of current legislation and NCC guidance. In addition, they will need to assess the extent to which their current curriculum organization and management structures enable such policies to be realized in practice. This involves reviewing areas such as: academic/pastoral divisions; staffing structures; resourcing; strategies for planning within, between and across curriculum areas.

Conclusion

In this paper we have argued for the need for schools to develop whole-school curriculum planning in which the explicit provision for the personal and social development of pupils is central. We have suggested that the cross-curricular elements should play a major role in such initiatives but that the curriculum provision for these elements should be built on principles of coherence and challenge for pupils. We have briefly described a framework which we believe has the capacity to provide that coherence and challenge. This framework has begun to form the basis of new whole-school curriculum development within a number of LEAs and schools. We see the framework as one contribution to what we hope will be a new and sustained movement to develop a truly broad and balanced curriculum for all pupils.

14

A National Curriculum: the Place of Humanities

John Slater

Five main issues will be addressed: What *are* the humanities? What is their relationship? How effective are they? What are they for, and do they humanize?

The Issue of Definition

Humanities departments in schools almost invariably embrace the teaching of history, geography and religious education. In the recent past some departments also contained sociology and social studies until they became non-subjects in the National Curriculum, banned not by explicit and argued policy but by surreptitious cold-shouldering. (Where *did* that *Curriculum Matters* on social studies get to? Written it was, but never published.)

Humanities departments are arbitrarily exclusive. They exclude, in the main, language and literature, the creative arts, and the impact of science and technology on human lives. And what they *do* include, arguably, are not exclusively humanities. History certainly lies at the heart of human studies, and religious education is concerned with deep and universal human experiences and aspirations. But geography? When the Final Report of the Geography Working Party was published its members saw their natural allies as scientists not as historians. Not all geographers share this view and their camp is divided. So humanities departments do not contain all those subjects concerned with human behaviour, and one of its principal members is unsure whether it *is* a humanity. Let us see 'humanities' as a flag of convenience carrying different cargoes to different destinations.

Some humanities departments, or 'faculties' as they often term themselves, are purely administrative alliances and none the worse for that. Subjects are taught separately, with a faculty head, a post sometimes created specifically to keep a good teacher in the classroom by giving him or her an enhanced post. Certainly a device with some merit. Some faculties have the additional function of giving single person departments, often battered, non-specialist, conscripted teachers of religious education, the support and security of a team. Faculties may have adjacent classrooms and a shared office, even a shared departmental capitation. But essentially they have managerial not curricular functions.

The Issue of Relationships

But once the relationship between humanities subjects are defined and extend beyond mere coexistence, the faculty acquires a *curricular* function. Is the relationship integrated, interdisciplinary, cross-disciplinary, or modular? By 'integrated' I mean a curriculum which submerges subjects and synthesizes them into a new discipline. It is a model defended by those who see knowledge as a 'seamless web', and are suspicious of what they often term 'traditional subject barriers'. 'Interdisciplinary' describes distinct subjects, usually history and geography, working together, using their complementary and contrasting procedures and skills, to study a topic of common interest, say, the changing nature of a village, suburb or region. 'Cross-disciplinary' more appropriately describes situations where, in the main, subjects are taught separately but establish an alliance to identify and teach themes that cross subject boundaries, for example, 'economic understanding' or 'citizenship'. A 'modular' course contains quite distinct units or modules of, say, history or geography. Often they contain a prescribed common core to ensure that both subjects are studied by all students but this is accompanied by a menu selected by the students which can be, for example, divided equally between the two subjects, or produce a course that is predominantly either historical or geographical. In the appendix of DES (1985b) details were given of such a course being taught successfully in a Wiltshire comprehensive school.

All these four models are joint courses. Their shared quality is that they oblige teachers to think *ecumenically*, to plan and evaluate their work as teams, and deepen the understanding of their own specialism by defining its relationship with those of their colleagues.

In 1990 John MacGregor retreated from guaranteeing a broad humanities curriculum for all pupils up to the age of 16, in a decision described in the *Independent* (2 August 1990), as a move which 'threatens history, widely accepted as one of the fundamentals of a good basic education. He is approaching that ill-defined line beyond which pragmatic flexibility becomes a retreat from essentials.' Geography and the arts were also casualties of this retreat. It returned to the nonsense of pupils' beginning to specialize at the age of 14, of history and geography being seen as interchangeable humanities, and of the abandonment of one of the great strengths of a national curriculum, the defining of an entitlement curriculum for all.

Humanities alliances have the potential merit of maintaining the study of history and geography for all pupils up to the age of 16. Key Stage 4 remains clogged, possibly unteachable, and is still a hypothesis waiting to be tested.

Content increases. Time does not. However, Model 2 in the Statutory Instruments offers the possibility of slimmed down courses in history and geography which might provide the basis for a workable humanities alliance. They would also exemplify the requirements of the National Curriculum to explore links between subjects, although the Statutory Instruments and the NCC's non-statutory guidance are better at applauding the idea than on the practical problems of implementing it. Neither the working groups nor the NCC demonstrated in their own procedures the kind of co-operation which they demanded of others.

The History and Geography Working Parties met separately, neither were obliged to consult during their proceedings, nor did they do so. There was no attempt to co-ordinate their working timetables or to publish their reports at the same time. The historians welcomed links with geography. The geographers spurned those with history. References in the two reports to subject links read like tagged on after-thoughts. Perhaps their hearts were not in it.

There has always been a suspicion of humanities courses in what was then the DES, fed to some extent by the evidence of HMI, whose doubts about humanities courses were not an objection in principle but about observed practice. But there *were* effective courses. What explained them?

The Issue of Effectiveness

First, the courses were taught by teachers more than usually aware of the particular procedures and skills of their own subjects. They were up-to-date with the implications of curriculum developments such as the Schools History Project and Geography for the Young School Leaver. In other words they believed in and understood the distinct characteristics of separate subjects. Their courses were in other words, *interdisciplinary or modular and not integrated*. No talk from them of 'seamless webs'!

Undoubtedly a potential strength of humanities teams is the curriculum development that can take place *between* subjects; the best recognize that this is no substitute for developments *within* subjects. The best geographers know that they cannot understand the physical environment and its impact on the lives of people unless they understand how they have changed through time. The best historians know that they cannot understand the behaviour of people in the past unless they appreciate the impact on it of the physical environment. When a teacher of history talks about the environment she is not becoming a temporary geographer; when a geographer talks about human behaviour changing over time he is not for the moment abandoning geography. They have both become better historians and geographers. And those seismic changes in the learning of history and geography – the Schools History Project and Geography for the Young School Leaver – developed from within distinct subjects.

Second, the schemes of work justified themselves, not primarily because they were part of a humanities alliance, but because the subject matter was worth learning. Three subjects in search of a theme are led by ideology, not learning. Humanities is a strategy, a curricular device, not a crusade or a doctrine. A history of the English landscape (one of the best interdisciplinary courses I observed) demanded an alliance between history and geography, whereas another on Elizabethan England or the origins of the Second World War would not. Often a humanities alliance makes sense to support a topic, or particular theme, but not necessarily for a whole course.

Third, successful courses were the result of considerable planning, say, minimally for a year, and regular subsequent evaluation. For this they depended on the support of head teachers insisting on timetabled planning and evaluation meetings. Effective courses had active support of heads who not only were committed to the curricular aims of the humanities course, but were aware of the complexities of their implementation.

Fourth, success depended as much on the instinctive ecumenical temperaments and friendships of the teachers as much as it did on the qualities of their teaching. One triumphantly successful course had its origins in a group of history and geography teachers who were already good friends and who drank in the same pub.

Fifth, joint courses flourished best when their constituent parts were taught by the appropriate specialists, historians or geographers or whatever. Subject specialists have enough to do to keep up with their own subjects and the demands made on them by the National Curriculum, without having to cope with another. Such arrangements have more ideological than curricular justification. They were responsible for many good teachers teaching badly and, incidentally, the floundering of many student teachers. Indifferent geography taught by good history teachers, and vice-versa, is a wasteful use of scarce resources.

It follows that the *practical* support of head teachers is crucial, that joint-courses imposed from above on teachers unused to working or unable to work as a team may not work, and that humanities courses based on assumptions more often asserted than examined, have weak foundations. Two in particular need to be re-examined. One is that subjects are artificial, and 'that children do not think naturally in terms of subjects'. Well, they do not think naturally in terms of the French language or the twelve-times table. But that is no argument against studying the one or learning the other. These comments are unapologetically and, for reasons of space, assertively Hirstian.

The other assumption behind many humanities courses is that the change from primary to secondary education is 'traumatic', so that pupils need to be eased into secondary education with an integrated humanities curriculum and a form-teacher based organization. There seems scant evidence for the existence of this trauma or its remedy. (Indifferent teaching and uncaring teachers are much more likely to be traumatic.) Problems are more likely to occur because secondary-trained teachers attempt to teach in a style and organization with which they are unfamiliar.

So far this article has considered the context of humanities courses as they are generally seen in schools, that are centred around some kind of joint arrangement between history and geography. The rest will be focused on history, because that is what I know a little more about.

The Issue of Function

Central to the argument of John White and Philip O'Hear is that the aims of a National Curriculum should be 'based on the promotion of students' well-being, not in any egoistic sense, but as citizens of a liberal democratic society' (O'Hear and White 1991). But it is not an *intrinsic* aim of history to support or create a liberal democratic society. Intrinsic aims include, for example, knowing the difference between AD and BC, having some understanding and knowledge about the origins and outcomes of the two World Wars, being able to evaluate critically evidence of human behaviour, understanding key historical concepts such as 'cause' and 'change', insisting that statements made about human beings are consistent with available evidence and linked to it with what we can call 'rational thought'. To promote particular kinds of societies or transmit values can be, perhaps, *educational* aims, but they are extrinsic to history. (These issues are debated at greater length in Lee *et al.* (1992).)

Of course history cannot separate itself from the values and ethics of the society in which it is learnt. Here it is perhaps helpful to make another distinction: between what history seeks to *guarantee*, and what it may potentially *enable*. It seeks to guarantee some knowledge and understanding of past societies, including the historical context of our own, and the ability to think historically about human behaviour. This may enable some of its students to become, say, professional historians, or to enjoy a lifelong love of the past – its battlefields, architecture, canals and railways – or to study black or feminist history, to become more informed and reflective politicians, lawyers, business people or head teachers, or to extend the insights of sociologists, geographers, philosophers, to become more reflective and informed Marxists, advocates of world citizenship, monetarists or gay rights campaigners. But it does not *seek* any of these outcomes.

What lies at the heart of historical thinking is the examination of values, not their transmission. Thus, it is essentially a mind-opening, not a socializing, subject. It demonstrates that shared evidence is often subject to different interpretations. It presents its students with apparently simple issues, with tidy and confident moral judgements – six causes of the Russian Revolution, the 'free world' and 'the Evil Empire', heroes and heroines, cowboys and

Indians, socialism and the free market – and shows that behind the confident explanations and comfortably categorized judgements are exceptions, subtleties, uncertainties. Ultimately historical statements are tentative and provisional. Historical thinking explores, but rarely reaches destinations. It examines but does not solve problems. History cannot claim to offer complete knowledge or total understanding. History asserts the status of doubt. But it is neither value-free nor politically neutral. As history challenges stereotypical thinking and prejudice, it is unlikely to flourish in authoritarian societies or to be welcomed by closed minds. If historical thinking does not seek to support or establish a liberal democratic society, it is certainly one of its symptoms.

The Issue of Humanizing

But does history *humanize*? Simply knowing about the past does not. The past is well-remembered in Serbia and Croatia and in Northern Ireland. But this is the past conscripted to *transmit* values, to mobilize loyalties. It is a past linked too firmly to knowledge, too deferential to political control.

History will humanize, if we are lucky and do not drop our guards, if: it continues to challenge stereotypical thinking and prejudice; it seeks not just to know about human behaviour but to reflect critically about it (provided, that is, the National Curriculum does not allow the weighting of its Attainment Targets and particularly its assessment procedures to enhance the status of knowledge at the expense of critical skills);[1] it can allow its students some appreciation of the worth and roots of themselves not only as individual human beings, but as members of a culture and a community (provided, that is, centralized uniform syllabuses do not ride roughshod over the variety of geographical, cultural, ethnic and social circumstances in which it is studied);[2] it can encourage young people to understand something of the attitudes and predicaments of people different from themselves (provided, that is, that pressures on Ministers do not persuade them that historical imagination and empathy are threats to the discipline of history rather than central to it); it can empower young people by lessening their ignorance and misunderstanding of, and helping to clarify their confusions about, the world they live in by putting it in its historical context of change through time (provided, that is, ill-informed and silly Ministers do not place obstacles to the historical study of the recent past); and the assessment of history can give parity of esteem to young people working collaboratively, talking in groups, with those writing in silence as competitive individuals (provided, that is, assessment does not become dominated by tests led by the need to produce easily measurable scores and please the Chairman of SEAC).

The outlook is not too encouraging. The ultimate control is not just central, but political. Recent appointments to what were once proudly independent professional bodies have been overtly political and have corrupted the educational debate.

Three Remaining Questions[3]

The questions are concerned with: the level of children's understanding; the openness of the historians' agenda; the effect on society of historical thinking.

First, as history is concerned with provisional and tentative statements, with problems that have no solutions, with questions which may have more than one answer, with establishing doubt, are we not seriously underestimating the need for clarity, predictability and certainty in the learning particularly of younger children? There is no confident answer but such evidence that my HMI colleagues had suggests that there is no serious problem, provided that is, that teachers are aware of its existence.

Language has to be accessible; it may have to be simplified. This does not mean that the intellectual demand has correspondingly to be lowered. Rather is it the opposite. It may well be that the issue is less one of age and intelligence than of temperament. There are adults as well as children who are drawn more to predictability, precision and problem-solving; others to ambiguity, puzzles and mysteries. The task is not to exempt either from ways of thinking they do not find easy but to encourage their access to them.

Second, how open is the historians' agenda? In an open society – one in which plurality is seen not as a problem but welcomed as a quality – we are surely not in the business of restricting choice? (Although there may be some teachers of history who still lurk in an illiberal closet and would feel discomfited by students campaigning on behalf of gay rights or studying gay history.) But what of a pupil who thanked us because history had enabled him to become a more informed member of the British Movement, or had made her a more confident racist? Are we right to feel uneasy? By what criteria? There are two. I have space to do little more than assert them. The first is historical. Historical thinking is hostile to prejudice and racial stereotyping as is the historians' insistence that statements about individuals, groups and whole cultures must be consistent with available evidence. There is no evidential basis for racism. That is no more negotiable than is '$12 \times 12 = 144$'. We cannot prevent our pupils joining the British Movement. But history cannot be used as their justification. Second, there are also sound educational reasons for our disquiet. We are all concerned with pupils in schools. Schools are to enable pupils to learn. Thus they must strive to be havens. They will fail if any of their learners feel threatened or undervalued. A school fails, contradicts its calling, if it seems to endorse, even indirectly, prejudice and discrimination. The liberal agenda is not boundless.

The third question concerns the aims and consequences of historical thinking. It is proper to ask how societies can survive without decisions being taken and problems solved, if confident statements are always tempered with doubt, if the need to judge is blunted by an awareness of alternative verdicts, and all encouraged by history. But historical thinking is only one strand of thinking. History is rational, demands evidence, and accepts alternative interpretations based on it. On the other hand, political thinking (as opposed to political education), for example, is concerned with the organization of one partial point of view.

Governments and civil servants and soldiers *have* to take decisions usually without having solved problems. Religious belief is not authenticated by evidence in the historical sense, nor is the love between two people or the emotional impact of great art; mathematics and science demand a greater degree of predictability. Constitutionally, liberal democratic societies depend on a separation and a *balance* of powers. None dominates. All contribute. So it is with patterns of thinking. Historical thinking does not dominate, but without it, pupils, and an open society, will be disabled.

I wish I felt more confident that our National Curriculum and its policy guardians will safeguard, or even understand, the humanizing role of humanities. We must accept the existence of the National Curriculum, but not uncritically and certainly not with deference. Too much is at stake.

Notes

1 Was the Geography Working Party not worried about this? Or were they unaware of the problem? Or did they suffer from a nasty attack of deference?
2 We have allowed ourselves to accept that a National History Curriculum had to mean one centralized history syllabus.
3 This section is drawn largely from Slater (1992).

15

A Primary Perspective on the National Curriculum

Barbara MacGilchrist

This paper represents a personal view. Whilst it draws on recent reports and research evidence it also incorporates knowledge gained from working directly in and with schools. It examines the impact of the National Curriculum on primary education in general, primary schools in particular and last, but by no means least, on the children themselves. It argues that with the introduction of the National Curriculum and the accompanying assessment requirements some significant changes are taking place in primary education, but the extent to which these changes are likely to have a positive impact on levels of achievement is yet to be determined. It raises issues of concern for the future.

The National Curriculum and Primary Education

The sequential introduction of the National Curriculum subjects, and for Key Stage 1 teachers the early requirement to do SATs, has had a significant impact in a number of respects. The whole profile of primary education has been raised which has resulted in a public, and more importantly, a political spotlight being focused on primary schools and those who teach in them in a way not seen since the Plowden Report in the 1960s (CACE 1967). With the introduction of the National Curriculum, primary schools are no longer seen politically as different from secondary schools. They are expected to teach a set range of subjects and will be judged by learning outcomes in relation to those subjects. The publication of the Key Stage 1 SAT results has led to questions being raised about not just what teachers should teach but how they should teach. The 'real books' debate, the publicity surrounding the Leeds evaluation exercise (Alexander 1991), and the publication of the recent Department for Education discussion paper on primary education (DES 1992a) are all symptomatic of this noticeable shift in emphasis.

A major impact of the National Curriculum therefore is that it has acted as a catalyst for challenging some fundamental beliefs and values about primary education. It has touched the very culture of primary schools. A culture that until recently had as its focus the child and the learning process; a culture in which how children learn was seen as more important than the content of that learning. A culture expressed through the centrality of the class teacher system. Given that culture, the National Curriculum was seen by many as a threat to 'good primary practice' – a term often used but rarely defined. No longer can the aims of primary education be taken as read. The stage is set for a redefinition, for a clarification, about the purposes of primary education. This is a welcome challenge providing the debate reflects not just the National Curriculum as it is now but projects ahead to the likely requirements of primary education in the twenty-first century. In the absence of such forward thinking a utilitarian definition could emerge that denigrates the past, traps primary education in the present and fails to open doors to the future.

The National Curriculum and Schools

From the reports and limited research evidence available, it would seem that the National Curriculum has had a differential impact on primary schools. Some schools have found the National Curriculum and assessment arrange-ments difficult to accommodate to, not least because of the challenge of having to manage multiple innovations imposed from outside. Whilst past attempts to change the curriculum of schools from outside were non-statutory in nature, the lessons learnt cannot be ignored. The rapid introduction of the National Curriculum, coupled with the relentless undermining of the work of primary schools in the media, has tended to shake the confidence of primary teachers. This has placed some schools in a defensive, reactive mode; not a conducive climate within which to bring about successful change. On the other hand some schools have grown in confidence. They have used the National Curriculum to strengthen and make more rigorous the whole-school approaches to curric-ulum planning and assessment they were developing anyway. Ironically there is a potential danger that we could see a widening of the gap between the most and least effective schools as far as the quality of the curriculum and the way it is organized is concerned. This is likely to have an impact on the quality of pupil learning in those schools.

Over and above these general statements some more specific comments can be made about the impact of the National Curriculum in schools from two perspectives: the *intended* and the *offered* curriculum. The National Curric-ulum has had a noticeable effect on the intended curriculum of primary schools, namely the declared, written intentions a school makes in the form of policy statements and guidelines. No longer do primary teachers have to invent the curriculum. The National Curriculum has offered a much needed framework and has provided an opportunity for removing the 'curriculum lottery' that existed in the past between schools and between classes in the same school. There is evidence from HMI reports that teachers have worked hard to come to terms with the National Curriculum (DES 1991a). It has stimulated and strengthened team work, whole-school planning, record keeping and assessment procedures and some schools have developed new, imaginative and flexible planning arrangements.

But, despite early guidance from the NCC on a framework for the primary curriculum (NCC 1989), the piecemeal approach to the National Curriculum and the lack of overall coherence has made it very difficult for primary schools to develop a curriculum planning framework that incorporates the National Curriculum and other learning experiences outside the statutory orders. The fact that the goalposts keep changing has added to the problem. Primary schools are now faced with curriculum overload. The present reality is that Key Stage 2 teachers potentially have to take account of up to 486 statements of attainment. This illustrates the dangers of over-prescription of the curriculum. It has caused many primary schools to engage in very complex curriculum planning devices which can have the effect of fragmentation rather than unification of the curriculum on offer.

From the perspective of the offered curriculum, namely the learning opportunities actually provided in the classroom, the National Curriculum has been responsible for a number of changes. Much more time is being spent on planning and assessment although attainment targets are driving the planning. The use of programmes of study to assist with the development of schemes of work is still in its infancy. 'Mopping up' uncovered attainment targets in the summer term is not uncommon.

The most noticeable impact has been the rapid expansion of science. When science came on the planning agenda, teachers found they could adapt their topic plans accordingly. From 1990 science-related topics became the norm. The extent to which the focus has now switched to history and geography remains to be seen. With the bolt-on introduction of the National Curriculum it would be interesting to know if science has now gone 'off the boil'.

It could be argued that the introduction of history and geography has been a watershed in primary schools in terms of how teaching and learning is organized. The amount of content to be covered across a growing number of subjects requires a fundamental rethink about past approaches to curriculum planning and curriculum organization. The tenacious adherence by primary teachers to 'topic work', which itself is often ill-defined and means different things to different teachers, needs to be challenged. No longer can an umbrella approach to curriculum planning be sustained whereby one theme can act as a catalyst to draw together different and often incoherent strands of the curriculum. More imaginative and focused approaches to integrated studies are required.

The Department for Education (DFE) primary discussion document, notwithstanding the media hype, has raised some very important questions that certainly do need to be addressed. For example: the place of integrated work and how it is planned; the place of subject teaching; the use of subject expertise amongst the teaching staff; the viability of one teacher per class for the year; the availability of subject expertise; the need for more flexible approaches to learning and the nature of the balance between whole-class, group and individual teaching. It is essential that this debate is entered into. The National Curriculum provides an opportunity to rethink, to throw off some of the shackles of the past that in part have been derived from dogmatic views about teaching and learning. Handled well, the debate could lead to even more enriched curriculum experiences for children. The maxim in the DFE discussion document of 'fitness for purpose' is not a bad starting point.

The debate about primary practice ignores at its peril the realities of primary schools. Creating the time needed for planning, developing and sharing subject expertise is essential. The demands of the National Curriculum have increased, not diminished, the planning and assessment time needed by teachers. Building in staffing flexibility is a must if changes in teaching are to be realized. This means that the issue of non-contact time, or rather the lack of it, has to be addressed. The last staffing survey was done in 1988. It revealed that primary class teachers had on average less than 8 minutes a day non-contact time. That was unacceptable then, and if the situation is no different now, it is untenable. As a starting point an updated staffing survey is needed along with an urgent view of formula funding for primary schools. The differential impact of the present formula funding arrangements on primary schools in relation to real staff costs needs to be investigated. Secondary schools have a long history of curriculum-led funding. It is no longer tenable, given the demands of the National Curriculum, to have what is now a very false divide between primary and secondary schools in relation to curriculum funding. To argue that the curriculum needs of a Year 6 child are fundamentally different from those of a Year 7 child can no longer be sustained. At a minimum primary schools should have activity-led funding. This would give schools the scope needed to argue for additional funding for resources to support the curriculum on offer in the school and the particular learning needs of children. Reading Recovery would be just one example of a curriculum activity that could and should attract additional funding.

School-based and school-focused inservice education play an important role in supporting the professional development of teachers. There is also a need to ensure that quality inservice education is available outside the school not least to extend the subject knowledge of primary teachers. However, the ability of LEAs to offer advisory support is diminishing and any one primary school gets only a small slice of the Grants for Education Support and Training (GEST) cake because of the number of schools involved and the number of teachers looking for and needing a share of that cake. School-controlled inservice development is to be encouraged and welcomed but the danger of schools 'recycling their own inadequacies' has already been highlighted in the DFE discussion document.

The National Curriculum and Children

It is relatively easy to comment on the impact of the National Curriculum at the level of whole-school policies and classroom practice; it is much more difficult to assess the impact of the National Curriculum from the perspective of the *received curriculum*, namely what the children are getting out of it at the end of the day. What can be said is that it is too soon to say very much. From experience and from research evidence, the length of time it takes to bring about educational change, especially when that change is top down, is well known (Fullan and Steigelbauer 1991). In the short term it can be argued that children are experiencing more science than in previous years. The same is likely to be true of history and geography. Key Stage 1 SAT results are now available. Despite the negative comments expressed in the media and political arenas they were hardly surprising and represent, notwithstanding their criterion-referenced focus, a normal curve of distribution.

But, in the long term, the impact is unknown. What we do know from the last HMSCI Report (DES 1992b) is that in terms of overall standards, nothing has changed so far compared with previous years. 70% of work seen in 1990/1 was satisfactory or better; 30% still unsatisfactory. In schools with disadvantaged intakes the results were even less satisfactory. By way of example, at Key Stage 2 in schools with disadvantaged intakes only 55% of the work seen was satisfactory. This correlates with research evidence demonstrating the persistent and consistent underachievement of children, particularly in inner city areas. The extent to which the National Curriculum in its present form can address this problem is open to question.

The HMSCI Report and the DFE discussion document have focused attention on standards. The latter document quotes evidence to show that standards in English and mathematics may be falling. The validity of the evidence is of course open to scrutiny and question, but nevertheless any suggestion of such a trend must be taken seriously. Such evidence cannot be divorced from issues to do with the problems of curriculum content overload now facing primary teachers. There have already been suggestions for example that time for the teaching of reading is being squeezed out. At all costs there is a need to avoid a 'kneejerk' reaction such as happened with the SATs which in some cases have now been reduced to little more than paper-and-pencil tests which, unlike some of the original imaginative mathematics and science SATS, are likely to narrow rather than widen learning opportunities for children.

The Secretary of State has announced that there is to be a review of the content of the National Curriculum at the primary level. It could be argued that a way of resolving the problem of curriculum overload is to simply reduce the curriculum to a narrow core of subjects in primary schools. Any such move would need to be thought through very carefully as it could negate the fundamental principle of 'entitlement' to a broad, balanced curriculum for all children that was built into the National Curriculum legislation in the first place. A more profitable starting point would be to reconsider the breadth and balance of curriculum opportunities that children need to have access to across the 7 years of primary schooling. To begin with there could be a stronger focus on literacy and numeracy in the early years to ensure that children acquire the skills needed to have access to a broad curriculum as quickly as possible. Such a suggestion is not as outrageous as it might first seem. Ask any teacher of nursery and infant children what their key priorities are. High on the list will be the need to ensure that children become competent readers and writers and are numerate. Ask any nursery and infant teacher how this can best be achieved and the vast majority will say not through a narrow skills-based programme unrelated to children's everyday experiences. Quite the reverse, teachers will stress the importance of children developing such skills in a real context so that they come to understand their purpose and range of uses. For young children the main context will be a study of themselves and their local environment. In this way children can develop a sense of place, of change over time and of how things work. Ideas can be developed and represented through the creative and expressive arts. At all times however the focus of attention in these early years should be the development of literacy and numeracy skills with learning to read a top priority. The availability of quality time in key areas of learning in the early years will pay dividends in the later years of primary education. At Key Stage 2, children will be ready to acquire some of the key concepts, skills and ideas underpinning different subject areas. Quality of thinking and understanding, not quantity of subject matter, should be the aim. This more focused curriculum offer would lay firm foundations for secondary education. Such a focus should help combat underachievement and reduce the unacceptably high numbers of children in Key Stage 2 and beyond who are unable to take advantage of the curriculum opportunities on offer.

Some Final Thoughts

At the end of the day it is teachers in classrooms deciding the next learning step for each child who will determine the success or otherwise of any national curriculum. There is a real need to stop undermining teachers and to seek instead positive, constructive ways of enhancing their professionalism. In turn teachers will be better placed to enhance learning opportunities for children and raise levels of achievement. In 1987 the National Curriculum 5 to 16 Consultation Document confirmed that 'Legislation alone will not raise standards. The imaginative application of professional skills at all levels of the education service within a statutory framework which sets clear objectives will raise standards' (DES 1987a). This should remain a guiding principle, as the National Curriculum is reshaped to take account of the present realities and future requirements of primary education.

16

Shaping the 14–19 Curriculum

Michael Young

Introduction

The problem with the 14–19 curriculum in this country is that except for the small, albeit rising, minority who go on to higher education, it does not exist. 40% do not continue after 16 and half of those remaining leave at 17 or before. Less than 30% achieve five or more GCSEs (Grade A–C) at 16 (less than half the number achieving a similar level in France and Germany) (Mortimore 1991). For those who achieve this level, A-levels provide a clear route of progression to higher education but little continuity as they pay little attention to the learning skills developed 14–16. For the remaining 70% there are the uncertain alternatives of either staying on at school and retaking GCSEs or taking one of the limited number of vocational courses that are available, or trying to get into a college.

This paper attempts to address the roots of these problems of low participation and low achievement, at least insofar as this can be attributed to the curriculum. It does this primarily by concentrating on the issues of continuity and progression at 16-plus. The paper is divided into four sections. Section 1 identifies a number of the curriculum factors associated with low achievement. Section 2 briefly examines recent Government policies and their possible effects. Section 3 argues that the fundamental question for the future of the 14–19 curriculum is whether divisions between the 'academic' and the 'vocational' at 16-plus are maintained or whether we should be envisaging a unified, but not uniform, 14–19 curriculum for all students. Some of the implications of the latter alternative are then explored, followed by consideration of the issues involved in building continuity through the 14–19 phase. The paper concludes in Section 4 that despite the divisive elements in recent Government policy, unifying curricular tendencies are also apparent. It is these tendencies which offer hope that the 14–19 curriculum of the future will, by being *more unified* and *more diverse*, be able to offer real opportunities for achievement to most if not all of the age cohort.

The Problems

The existing 14–19 curriculum is a product of its history. It is characterized by discontinuity and low levels of participation after 16, lack of relevance and incentives for the majority of learners, divisions (particularly after 16) and lack of flexibility for those who leave and want to return. The problems with the divided character of the 14–19 curriculum are comprehensively described and analysed in Finegold *et al.* (1990) who argue that the outcome is an exclusive and archaic academic route and a low status, low quality 'vocational' alternative. The authors make the case for a unified but flexible modular curriculum from 14-plus consisting of foundation and advanced stages and a Diploma normally achieved at 18 which would replace A-levels and current vocational qualifications.

Government Policy in Relation to the 14–19 Curriculum

Until very recently Government policy on the curriculum has been largely expressed through the National Curriculum and TVEI. The former is designed to ensure a broad subject-based curriculum for all up to 16, and the latter, by explicitly adopting a 14–18 framework and giving priority to overcoming divisions between academic and vocational programmes, emphasizes both continuity and relevance.

These ambitious aims of TVEI have been limited by the divided structure of qualifications (Spours and Young 1988, Spours 1992). Despite these constraints, however, TVEI was able to support a broadening of GCSE and A-levels and to encourage some programmes that combined academic and vocational courses.

Since 1991 Government policy on the curriculum has more explicitly emphasized divisions rather than integration as a way of improving standards, thus exaggerating tendencies which have a long history in English education. The specific policies were most clearly expressed in DES (1991d) and consisted of: (i) the decision to restrict the amount of assessed course work at GCSE and A-level to approximately 20%; (ii) the introduction of 'vocational' alternatives at 14; (iii) the creation of three alternative routes – A- and AS-levels, gNVQs and NVQs at 16-plus.

The consequence of such policies on assessment and qualifications will inevitably strengthen the selective function of examinations, thus minimizing progression possibilities at 16-plus and 18-plus. Likewise, the new tripartite structure at 16-plus, with each 'track' embodying distinctive assessment regimes, will limit higher levels of both participation and achievement.

Continuity 14–19 and Division at 16-plus

In a recent paper Alison Wolf (1992) summarizes the problems we have inherited as follows:

> *education and training . . . [has been] characterised by an unusual and definitive split between pre and post-compulsory schooling. Up to 16, there [has been] a clear structure . . . of authority, organisation and certification. Beyond that date, a defined pre-university 'stream' existed alongside extremely diverse alternative provision which lacked any clear overall framework or oversight body.*

In other words it has been a system which has assumed that those who stay on at 16 are aiming for HE and the remainder have left. This is despite the fact that the former include no more than half of those still at school or college after 16. The most striking evidence for such an assumption is that the vast majority of programmes available for those over 16 (approximately 80%) are A-levels (examinations geared to only 20% of the cohort). It is not surprising that many of the 60% who now stay on at 16 leave at 17 or earlier without any qualifications at all. The GCSE examinations at 16-plus continue to have both a *terminal* (school-leaving certificate) and *selective* role. They thus limit continuity in the 14–19 phase for all except the 25% who are likely to achieve high level passes in GCSE at 16.

Achieving continuity from 14–19 involves a shift from a system geared to selection to one which gives priority to standards and to participation – in other words a *mass high-achievement system*. Such a system goes against the grain of English educational history, and will involve a number of issues that I can do no more than refer to in this paper. The issues that I shall consider are assessment, content and structure, common learning processes and the relationships between institutions. Finally I shall examine the potential for continuity of a number of recent post-16 developments.

Assessment

With the greater priority given in recent years to comparing educational systems, what stands out about the system in the UK is not only its domination by centrally controlled assessment but the extent to which assessment functions as a mechanism of selection and exclusion. The assessment issues in relation to enhancing 14–19 continuity are:

(i)   How is it possible to reduce the dominance of selection at 16 while at the same time maintaining standards?

(ii) Are externally assessed examinations at 16-plus necessary at all?

(iii) How can records of achievement be used to enhance progression and continuity across the 16-plus barrier? (Young 1993).

Structure and Continuity in the 14–19 Curriculum

The present structure offers minimal choice up to 16 through the National Curriculum and, depending on a student's GCSE grades, a highly structured choice between three kinds of route at 16-plus. Within the three routes, choice is dependent on what the local institutions are able to provide. The idea of continuity for all from 14–19 raises a number of questions which within the existing system have hardly even been envisaged. For example:

What should be the balance between compulsion and choice before and after 16?

Should all students have a curriculum that combines discipline-based study with practical applications?

How can the advantages of flexibility that a modular structure brings be maximized without the tendency to fragmentation inherent in modular structures? These issues are explored in both Finegold (1990) and in a number of the contributions to Young and Watson (1992).

Learning Processes

One of the most lasting effects of TVEI on the 14–19 curriculum is likely to be the recognition that improving achievement is as much about encouraging more effective learning as it is about reforming curriculum content. This focus is expressed in the priority given in TVEI to the idea of active learning and has led to more integrated careers education and guidance, individual action planning and support for records of achievement. Because they can be integrated across both academic and vocational routes, they have the potential to enhance progression and continuity across the 14–19 phase as a whole.

Institutional Competition and Collaboration

The 14–19 curriculum is shaped as much by organizational factors as by those specific to the curriculum itself. Although the vast majority of those between 14–16 are still held in LEA secondary schools, the situation after 16 becomes much more complex (Kidd 1992), when students are divided roughly equally between those still in school and those in college. This organizational fragmentation will become more marked as a result of the incorporation of colleges and the growth of the number of secondary schools opting for grant maintained status. Funding arrangements will inevitably lead to competition between institutions. While this may increase short-term participation, it will be unlikely to do the same for progression and continuity.

In what will be an increasingly divided institutional context, and with diminishing LEA support, schools will face enormous difficulties in delivering a broad based curriculum after 16. At best sixth forms will offer (in addition to

A-levels) some of the gNVQ routes such as health and caring, and business administration which makes least demands on technical resources and specialist staff.

It is difficult to see how real continuity and progression within the 14–18 phase can be guaranteed by individual sixth forms. Schools and colleges will need to collaborate closely together, through progression agreements, franchising of courses and modules and the use of records of achievement. Without the mediating role of LEAs and with the running down of TVEI, such collaboration is going to depend increasingly on the vision of heads and principals who see beyond the short-term advantages of competition.

Current Developments Post-16-gNVQs and the Advanced Diploma

DES (1991d) heralded substantial changes in the qualification system which will shape any reforms of the 14–19 curriculum in the next few years. Two major innovations are proposed – the *general vocational qualifications* framework for all non-A-level qualifications for full-time students and the overarching *Advanced Diploma* which will be obtainable through either academic or vocational qualifications. Potentially the Advanced Diploma has great possibilities. It could act as a framework for students to record and accumulate credit for a wide range of achievements and could be the basis for establishing continuity between post-16 qualifications and Key Stage 4 of the National Curriculum. Since the formal announcements of the Diploma, however, very little has been heard of it.

The gNVQ framework is designed to include all full-time 'vocational' study in initially five broad occupational areas (these are planned to be extended to at least 12 in the next 2 years). The innovative element of the framework is that its unit structure will enable students to combine academic and vocational studies in ways which were hardly possible in the old Business and Technology Education Council (BTEC) National. Whether this potential will be realized will depend on how far the Examination Boards are encouraged to modularize A- and AS-levels.

Unifying Tendencies in the 14–19 Curriculum

This paper has set out to describe the main features of what is a fast changing reality – the 14–19 curriculum. It has argued that it has neither coherence nor continuity for the majority and is hindered by a divided qualification system and fragmented institutional provision. Furthermore it is difficult to see how current Government reforms will do other than exacerbate these difficulties. Nevertheless it would be a mistake to end on a pessimistic note. Government policies, for all the media attention they get, are only one of the forces shaping the curriculum and are themselves often contradictory. The curriculum is also the outcome of professional initiatives and the responses of institutions as well as the changing aspirations and expectations of young people themselves. Both teachers and young people respond not only to Government reforms but also to a changing and uncertain social and economic context.

I will refer briefly to two developments which reflect these responses and which could lead to pressures for a more coherent and unified 14–19 curriculum. The first is the response of the young people themselves. Whether it is only as a consequence of the recession and the absence of jobs or whether we are seeing a more fundamental cultural change in attitudes and aspirations, many more young people are staying on at school or college and fewer are joining training schemes such as YT which, regardless of their training content, are perceived as stigmatizing those who join them as being of limited capability when they apply for jobs.

The substantial increase in the proportion of young people who are beginning to see full-time 14–18 education as a normal expectation presents a new challenge to schools and colleges. Instead of having one sixth form class doing Certificate of Pre-Vocational Education (CPVE) or GCSE retakes and the remainder doing A-levels, an increasing proportion of those staying on will be looking for courses other than A-levels. How schools respond to this challenge, and whether they can devise delivery frameworks which maximize flexibility and choice and within which both A-level and non-A-level students can be included, is going to be a major factor determining the shape of the 14–19 curriculum of the future.

The other major change likely to effect the 14–19 curriculum is in the admission policies of universities and colleges of higher education as they respond to new funding arrangements and the demand to increase student numbers. This is already leading to the development of HE/school/college compacts, franchising agreements and more generally the blurring of distinctions between what have traditionally been the very separate sectors of secondary, further and higher education.

As universities recruit a higher proportion of students with qualifications other than A-levels, the major influence, i.e. the link between A-levels and admission to university, which maintains a divided 14–19 curriculum will be weakened. Although new status hierarchies within higher education will replace old, they will not be so clear cut. With 70% or more completing a 14–19 curriculum and over half of them going on to higher education, many without A-levels, the mystique of academic subjects will inevitably be weakened. The possibility of continuity in the 14–19 curriculum could even become a reality.

Conclusion: A 14–19 Curriculum – the Way Ahead

This paper began with the statement that a 14–19 curriculum has never existed in this country except for a minority. The single major change that we need to consider is that it must aim to be at least for 80–90% of the school population. This does not mean uniformity but a unified framework within which a diverse range of opportunities are encouraged. Nor does it mean that by keeping young people away from the labour market until 18 or 19 they are being kept 'in school' in the old sense. The extra years are an opportunity, among others, to tackle one of the great absences in the curricula of mass schooling of the past – an understanding of the economy and the changing nature of work. Para-doxically, as young people are more and more excluded from the labour market, relationships between employers and education need to be closer. This is not only because teachers need to know more about how work is changing but because it is in partnerships with employers that elements of a new curriculum will be developed.

The question of a common core and the balances between unity and diversity and compulsion and choice goes beyond work and the economy. The curriculum issue is how, regardless of students' choices of programmes, they are prepared to be active citizens in a democracy. In attempting to devise a democratic 14–19 curriculum, it is unlikely that the insular specialization of either academic subjects or occupational preparation will have a place. Both traditions will need critical evaluation in light of efforts to grasp the kind of capabilities young people will need in the future.

Acknowledgements

I should like to express my thanks to Ken Spours for help in the initial preparation of this paper. Some of the ideas which we have worked on together are expressed in Young and Spours (forthcoming, 1993).

References

Alexander, R.J. (1991) *Primary Education in Leeds* Twelfth and Final Report from the Primary Needs Independent Evaluation Project, University of Leeds.

Ashdown, R., Carpenter, B. and Bovair, K. (1991) *Curriculum Challenge.* Falmer Press, Lewes.

Bakhtin, M. (1981) In *The Dialogic Imagination: Four Essays by Bakhtin*, (ed.) Michael Holguist. University of Texas, Austin.

Barlex, D. (1990) Using science and design and technology, *Design and Technology Teaching* Vol.22, No.3.

Barnett, M. (1992) Technology, within the National Curriculum and elsewhere, in J. Beynon and H. Mackay (eds.) *Technological Literacy and the Curriculum.* Falmer Press, Lewes.

Bernal, M. (1987) *Black Athena: The Afroasiatic Roots of Classical Civilisation.* Rutgers Press, New Brunswick.

Black, P. and Harrison, G. (1985) *In Place of Confusion: Technology and Science in the School Curriculum.* Nuffield-Chelsea Trust and National Centre for School Technology, London and Nottingham.

Blank, R.K. and Dalkilic, M. (1992) *State Policies on Science and Mathematics Education.* Council of Chief State School Officers, Washington DC.

British Association for the Advancement of Science (BAAS) (1889) Report of 59th meeting of the BAAS, Newcastle.

Brown, H. and Jones, S. (1939) *Introductory Applied Science* Vol.2. Macmillan, London

Buck, M. and Inman, S. (1992) *Whole School Provision for Personal and Social Development: the Role of Cross-Curricular Elements: Curriculum Guidance No.1*, Centre for Cross-Curricular Initiatives, Goldsmiths College, London.

Central Advisory Council for Education (CACE) (1967) *Children and their Primary Schools.* HMSO, London.

Editorial comment (1992) *Child Education* Vol.69 (8) p.4.

Clarke, K. (1991) *Education in a Classless Society*, The Westminster Lecture, given to the Tory Reform Group, June 1991.

Clifford, J. (1984) *The Predicament of Culture: Twentieth Century Ethnography, Literature and Art.* Harvard University Press, Cambridge.

Cohen, P. (1991) *Monstrous Images, Perverse Reasons: Cultural Studies in Anti-Racist Education.* Centre for Multicultural Education, University of London Institute of Education.

Council for Curriculum Reform (1945) *The Content of Education.* University of London Press, London.

Daniels, H. and Ware, J. (eds.) (1990) *Special Educational Needs and the National Curriculum: Impact of the Education Reform Act*, Bedford Way Series. Kogan Page, London.

Department of Education and Science (DES) (1977) *Curriculum 11–16.* HMSO, London.

DES (1978a) *National Survey of Secondary Education*, Her Majesty's Inspectorate. HMSO, London.

DES (1978b) *Special Educational Needs* (Warnock Report), Cmnd 7212.

DES (1985a) *Better Schools.* HMSO, London.

DES (1985b) *History in the Primary and Secondary Years: an HMI View.* HMSO, London.

DES (1987a) *The National Curriculum 5–16: A Consultation Document.* HMSO, London.

DES (1987b) Secretary of State's speech to the North of England Conference, DES Press Release.

DES (1988) *Task Group on Assessment and Testing: A Report.* HMSO, London.

DES (1989a) *National Curriculum: From Policy to Practice.* HMSO, London.

DES (1989b) *Science in the National Curriculum 1989.* HMSO, London.

DES (1991a) *The Implementation of the Curricular Requirements of ERA: an Overview by HM Inspectorate on the First Year, 1989–90.* HMSO, London.

DES (1991b) *Science in the National Curriculum 1991.* HMSO, London.

DES (1991d) *Education and Training for the 21st Century.* HMSO, London.

DES (1992a) *Curriculum Organisation and Classroom Practice in Primary Schools.* HMSO, London.

DES (1992b) *Education in England 1990–91: The Annual Report of HM Senior Chief Inspector of Schools.* HMSO, London.

DES (1992c) *Reporting Pupils' Achievements to Parents*, Circular 5/92. HMSO, London.

DES (1992d) *Statistical Bulletin 3/92.* HMSO, London.

DES (1992e) *The Parents' Charter: Publication of Information about School Performance in 1992*, Circular 7/92. HMSO, London.

DES (1992f) *Choice and Diversity: New Framework for Schools*, Cmnd 2021.

Education Reform Act 1988. HMSO, London.

Finegold, D. et al. (1990) *A British Baccalaureat.* Institute for Public Policy Research, London.

Fullan, M. (1982) *The Meaning of Educational Change*. Teachers College Press, Columbia University, New York.

Fullan, M.G. and Steigelbauer, S. (1991) *The New Meaning of Educational Change*. Cassell, London.

Further Education Unit and Engineering Council (FEU) (1988) *The Key Technologies: Implications for Education and Training*. Opus, Oxford.

Gifford, B.R. and O'Connor, M.C. (1992) *Changing Assessments: Alternative Views of Aptitude, Achievement and Instruction*. Kluwer, Boston and Dordrecht.

Gipps, C. (1992) National assessment: a research agenda, *British Educational Research Journal*, Vol.18, no.3.

Gundara, J. (1990) Societal diversities and the issue of 'The Other'. *Oxford Review of Education* Vol.16, No.1.

Hacker, A. (1992) *Two Nations: Black and White Separate, Unequal and Hostile*. Scribner, New York.

Kidd, L. (1992) In Young, M. and Watson, J. *Beyond the White Paper: the Case for a Unified System at 16+*, Post 16 Centre Report No. 8. Institute of Education, London.

Kimbell, R. *et al.* (1991) *The Assessment of Performance in Design and technology*. Schools Examination and Assessment Council, London.

Koupat, A. (1992) *Ethnocriticism: Ethnography, History, Literature*. University of California Press, Bentley.

Kizol, J. (1991) *Savage Inequalities in Children in American Schooling*. Crown Publications, New York.

Lawton, D. (1973) *Social Change, Educational Theory and Curriculum Planning*. Hodder & Stoughton, London.

Lawton, D. (1989) *Education, Culture and the National Curriculum*. Hodder & Stoughton, London.

Layton, D. (1988) Revaluing the T in STS. *International Journal of Science Education* Vol.10.

Lee, P. *et al.* (1992) *The Aims of School History: the National Curriculum and Beyond*, London File Series. Tufnell Press, London.

Lewis, A. (1991) *Primary Special Needs and the National Curriculum*. Routledge, London.

Longhorn (1991) A sensory Science curriculum, in Ashdown, R., Carpenter, B. and Bovair, K. (eds.) *Curriculum Challenge*. Falmer Press, Lewes.

McCulloch, G., Jenkins, E. and Layton, D. (1985) *Technological Revolution? The Politics of School Science and Technology in England and Wales Since 1945*. Falmer Press, Lewes.

Mortimer, J. (1991) *The Unqualified School Leaver*, Post 16 Education Centre Report No 9. Institute of Education, London.

National Curriculum Council (NCC) (1989) *Curriculum Guidance 1: A Framework for the Primary Curriculum*.

NCC (1990a) *The National Curriculum and Whole Curriculum Planning 1990*, Circular No.6.

NCC (1990b) *Curriculum Guidance Paper 3: The Whole Curriculum*.

NCC (1990d) *The Arts 5–16: A Curriculum Framework*. Oliver and Boyd, Harlow.

NCC (1992) *Curriculum Guidance Paper 9: National Curriculum and Pupils with Severe Learning Difficulties*.

National Union of Teachers (NUT) (1992) *Anti-Racist Curriculum Guidelines*.

Newsam, P. (1988) *Times Educational Supplement*, 29 December 1988.

Norwich, B. (1990) How an entitlement can become a constraint, in Daniels, H. and Ware, J. (eds.) *Special Education Needs and the National Curriculum: Impact of the Education Reform Act*, Bedford Way Series. Kogan Page, London.

Organisation for Economic Co-operation and Development (OECD) (1988) *School Development and New Approaches for Learning: Trends and Issues in Curriculum Reform*. OECD, Paris.

O'Hear, P. and White, J. (1991) *A National Curriculum for All: Laying the Foundation for Success*. Institute for Public Policy Research, London.

Ouvry, C. (1991) Access for pupils with profound and multiple learning difficulties, in Ashdown, R., Carpenter, B. and Bovair, K. (eds.) *Curriculum Challenge*. Falmer Press, Lewes.

Pascall, D. (1992) *Times Educational Supplement*. 29 May 1992. Times Supplements, 1992.

Plato *The Euthyphro*, in Hamilton, E. and Cairns, H. (eds.) (1963) *Plato: the Collected Dialogues*. Pantheon, New York.

Resnick, L.R. and Resnick, D.P. (1992) 'Assessing the thinking curriculum: new tools for educational reform' in Gifford, B.R. and O'Connor, M.C. (eds.) *Changing Assessments: Alternative Views of Aptitude, Achievement and Instruction*. Kluwer, Boston and Dordrecht.

Sebba, J. and Clarke, J. (1991) Meeting the needs of pupils within history and geography in Ashdown, R., Carpenter, B. and Bovair, K. (eds.) *Curriculum Challenge*. Falmer Press, Lewes.

Shelton, I. (1990) Social Science in the curriculum, *Social Science Teacher* Vol.20, No.1.

Shepard, L.A. (1992) Commentary: what policy makers who mandate tests should know about the new psychology of intellectual ability and learning, in Gifford, B.R. and O'Connor, M.C. (eds.) *Changing Assessments: Alternative Views of Aptitude, Achievement and Instruction*. Kluwer, Boston and Dordrecht.

Simon, B. (1992) *What Future for Education?* Lawrence and Wishart, London.

Slater, J. (1992) Where there is dogma, let us sow doubt, in Lee, P. et al. (eds.) *The Aims of School History: the National Curriculum and Beyond*, London File Series. Tufnell Press, London.

Smithers, A. and Robinson, P. (1992) *Technology in the National Curriculum*. The Engineering Council, London.

Spours, K. (1992) *Recent Developments in Qualifications at 14+ : a critical review*, Post 16 Education Working Paper, No. 12. Institute of Education, London.

Spours, K. and Young, M. (1988) Beyond vocationalism, *British Journal of Education and Work* Vol.2, No.2.

Times Educational Supplement (1992) Visions of chaos. Report of a speech by Professor Eric Bolton to the Council of Local Education Authorities, *TES* No.3970, 31 July 1992. Times Supplements, London.

Verma, S.L. (1986) *Towards a Theory of Positive Secularism*. Ramat Publications, Vaipur.

Whitty, G. (1990) The New Right and the National Curriculum: state control or market forces, in Hinde, M. and Hammer, M. (eds.) *The Education Reform Act, 1988: Its Origins and Implications*. Falmer Press, Basingstoke.

Williams, R. (1961) *The Long Revolution*. Penguin, London.

Wolf, A. (1992) *An assessment-driven system: education and training in England and Wales*, ICRA Working Paper No.3. Institute of Education, London.

Young, M. (1993) *Recording and Recognising Achievement in a Unified Curriculum*, Post 16 Education Working Paper No.13. Institute of Education, London.

Young, M. and Spours, K. (1993) *A Curriculum of the Future* (forthcoming).

Young, M. and Watson, J. (1992) *Beyond the White Paper: The Case for a Unified System at 16+*, Post 16 Centre Report No.8. Institute of Education, London.

Index